Take Me to the Cross

Take Me to the Cross

D E V O T I O N A L

Al Denson

Jeff Kinley

Tyndale House Publishers, Inc.
Wheaton, Illinois

Visit Tyndale's exciting Web site at www.tyndale.com

© 1997 by Al Denson. All rights reserved.

Designed by Paul Christenson
Edited by Lorraine Triggs

Cover photo from Al Denson's *Take Me to the Cross* album. This album is available on CD and cassette from Benson Records. Ask for it at any Christian bookstore.

Cover art direction: Mike Rapp and Rob Ascroft.
Cover photography: Matthew Barnes
Cover design: Ian Black
Photos of mission trip: Russ Busby

"Rain Love"
"Who'll Pray for Me"
"Right About Now"
"Fly with the Angels"
"Take Me to the Cross"
"The Choice"
"If You Believe in Miracles"
"If You Only Knew"
Words and Music by Al Denson, Robert White Johnson, and Chris Pelcer
© 1997 Paragon Music Corp. / ASCAP / RadioQuest Music Publishing / BMI / Million Suns Music / BMI / Al Denson Music / ASCAP. All rights reserved. Used by permission.

"The Road Less Travelled"
Words and Music by Lowell Alexander and Michael Gleason
© 1996 Sony / ATV Tunes LLC / Randy Cox Music, Inc. / BMI. All rights reserved. All rights admin. by Sony / ATV Music Publishing, 8 Music Square West, Nashville, TN 37203.

"Love Wants Nothing"
Words and Music by Lowell Alexander and Michael Gleason
© 1995 Sony / ATV Tunes LLC / Molto Bravo! Music, Inc. / ASCAP / Sony / ATV Songs LLC / Randy Cox Music, Inc. / BMI. All rights reserved. All rights admin. by Sony / ATV Music Publishing, 8 Music Square West, Nashville, TN 37203.

Scripture quotations are taken from the *Holy Bible*, New Living Translation, copyright © 1996. Used by permission of Tyndale House Publishers, Inc., Wheaton, Illinois 60189. All rights reserved.

ISBN 0-8423-7003-X

Printed in the United States of America

02 01 00 99 98
10 9 8 7 6 5 4 3

In Loving Memory of my friend Grant Milner,
Who died in our plane crash on December 18, 1994.
Because of Jesus, we don't have to say good-bye,
Just see ya' later.

Mission Statement

To be a creatively driven artist that will
lead the Christian music industry by
providing the public with an excellent message of Christ
through the talents God has given me.

To always live the words I write in my everyday life
through the actions I take and the words I speak.

To maintain a high level of integrity in my dealings with people
and always strive for excellence in everything I do,
as it is an expectation of myself and not just a goal.

Al Denson
Celebration Ministries

Contents

Foreword

Al Denson understands what it means to live and minister "in the trenches" for Christ. I have seen this firsthand as he has assisted us in our crusades and in crisis areas overseas.

Through his extensive and very effective outreach to youth—and through his own personal ordeal of surviving a plane crash but having to undergo numerous reconstructive surgeries on his face—Al has developed important insights into victorious discipleship.

In this book of devotions, *Take Me to the Cross,* Al will guide you through brief but rich times of Bible-centered thought and prayer. As you make use of this book, you'll grow and be strengthened as authentic followers of Christ.

Franklin Graham
Samaritan's Purse
Boone, North Carolina

Dear Friend,

You're about to begin a forty-five-day adventure of spending time alone with God! But why a forty-five-day devotional book? We believe that if you spend a little time each day with Jesus for—you guessed it—forty-five days, it will become a regular part of your life. And what could be a better habit to form than spending daily time with the Lord?

To get the most out of this book, use it with your Bible. As you look up the verses for the day, you'll be amazed at how much closer you will grow to the Lord. Writing down your thoughts and discoveries in the spaces provided will help you apply God's truths to your life. Each devotion takes about fifteen minutes, so be sure to carve out that time for you and the Lord.

We want you to enjoy being with Jesus and learning from his Word. So get started, and be ready to experience God in a new way. May the next forty-five days truly "take you to the cross"!

By his grace,
Al Denson and Jeff Kinley

Acknowledgments

It is very difficult to begin a page of thanks without first acknowledging the reasons for this writing. It's all because of Jesus Christ. First, to Jesus, I once again give you everything I have, everything I own, and ask for your continued blessing on what we do. Thank you, Lord, for my wife, Tracie, who has brought such peace and inspiration into my life. Thank you, Tracie, for standing by me, praying for me, and loving me. You are truly everything I ever wanted.

To my mother, father, brothers, Tracie's mom, and the entire family, who have been such a special part of our lives, I say thanks. You all need to know how much Tracie and I love you, and it's important to say that to you more often as we grow older together.

Our love for the church, my pastors, and fellow ministers grows every day. Sagemont Church in Houston has always been there for us. Now we are privileged to worship in Dallas with the great fellowship of Los Colinas. Thank you to all of the adopted churches around the world where we have had the honor to minister. You continue to make a difference in our lives. We give special thanks to the churches who are "Adopting an Artist" and pledging to pray for us as we minister on a daily basis.

Now to our team. Thank you, Kevin McAfee, for believing in me and encouraging me to create and write, write, write, and write some more. Your management and marketing skills are focused on evangelism and outreach ministry. May you and your family be blessed. Thank you to Wes Yoder, Tim Grable, and the Ambassador family for your sensitive nature to scheduling us in churches and venues across the globe. It has been such an incredible experience for all of us.

We also want to thank our sponsors. Rapha sponsors yearly "ministry events" and gives us the opportunity to take the name of Christ into places that others would not go. Thank you to Franklin Graham and Samaritan's Purse for your continued prayer and support. The opportunity to go to Bosnia was overwhelming, and Operation Christmas Child is now a part of our ministry! Thank you to UStel Long Distance Service for your support in our ministry.

Where would any ministry be without a Christ-centered board of advisors? Celebration Ministries has the best team of any ministry. These God-fearing men are Wes Christian, Don Sapaugh, Emory Gadd, Steve Tuggle, Stan Durham, George Gleason, and Tex Reardon. Your unceasing prayer support and leadership overwhelm us. We appreciate your expertise, love for God, personal sacrifice, and genuine vision for ministry.

We're grateful to The Benson Music Group, Bill Baumgart, Ken Pennell, Mike Rapp, Mark Campbell, Steve Fret, Melissa Hambrick, Mike Gay, Michael Burt, Zena Caruthers, Jeff Mosley, and the entire sales and distribution system. Thank you for being with me in my early years and seeing a future filled with promise.

Thank you to the Tyndale family. Our prayer is that we will make a lasting difference together.

Finally, I want to thank you for picking up this book. Now, you must take it with God's Word and meditate on how it can help you start over. It's time to begin something different, and you can start today. Forget about yesterday and don't worry about tomorrow. Let's find out together how you can make the right choices . . . from now on.

Introduction

How many times have you told friends that you would "touch base" with them later or said those far-too-familiar words "see ya tomorrow"? There is probably nothing more important to any relationship than taking the time for communication. While the subjects can get deeper sometimes, most of the time the conversations are about who likes whom, what is going on at school, and where we are going out this week, right? Everybody wants to "touch base" with a friend.

What happens when you're alone and there isn't a friend who will listen? That's what is great about "touching base" with someone who will always be there. His name is Jesus, and he's the "real deal." He really understands how you feel about everything that matters to you.

Whether you got this book at a concert, bought it at a bookstore, or received it as a gift, it all happened for a reason. All you need to do is decide that you'll try spending fifteen minutes a day with Al Denson's music, devotionals, and Bible readings, and you may just find yourself at the beginning of something dramatic in your universe.

You'll want to listen to the music from *Take Me to the Cross* as you do the studies in this book. The music is acoustic. It's upbeat, and so are the devotionals! Each day's study is quick, to the point, and centers around a central truth you can put to memory. Ask a friend to be your "accountability partner," or recruit your church youth group—just do it! The whole process will be a party!

Congratulations on taking this step—that's how the battle is won. When you give your life to Jesus, it not only can happen, it will happen! So what are you waiting for? It's time to get started!

Staying with the Stone,
Kevin McAfee
Celebration Ministries

CHAPTER ONE

Rain Love

Threw out my old raincoat
Set sail without a boat
For places somewhere far beyond my dreams

As the sky came pouring down
I laid down on the ground
Like I was dreamin'
I let the feelin' wash all over me

Chorus:
Rain—Rain Love
Comin' down all around me
Rain—Rain Love
So glad you finally found me
Rain—Rain Love
    (In time you're gonna recognize
    one drop will open up your eyes)
Love, Rain Love, Rain Love, Rain Love

It's the color of every sky
It's a wave to change the tide
When the world is crumbling down 'round you and me

It's the calm that lifts the storm
It's the promise that keeps you warm
When you don't understand
Just trust the guiding hand that calms the sea
It falls like

[repeat chorus]

Bridge:
Sometimes it takes the rain to make you realize
No greater love could ever fill the skies
God's love's the only reason why

What Do You Know? DAY 1

Rain Love

A teacher once quizzed a group of students about their knowledge of the Bible. Here are some of the answers the students came up with:

- Sodom and Gomorrah were boyfriend and girlfriend.
- Jezebel was Ahab's donkey.
- The New Testament Gospels were written by Matthew, Mark, Luther, and John.
- Eve was created from an apple.
- Jesus was baptized by Noah.

One of the best answers was given by a top student. The question: "What was Golgotha?" The answer: "Golgotha was the name of the giant who slew the apostle David."

If you've gone to church for a while, you probably laughed (or cried) at these answers. But we all have a lot to learn about the Bible. And when it comes to God's love, how much do we *really* know?

Today, look at a very familiar verse in your Bible—John 3:16. You've probably memorized this verse as a small child. But like many other things we're too familiar with in life, sometimes we can lose sight of its real meaning to us.

Read John 3:16 as if you are reading it for the first time. Use the following questions to help you think through it.

What does the phrase *the world* refer to?

3

What does the phrase *he gave his only Son* mean?

What do you think *so that* means?

In what way does this verse show love?

Now read John 3:16 again, and make it personal.

For God so loved _____ that he gave his only Son, so that [if] _____

believes in him _____ will not perish but have eternal life.

Has anybody ever come close to loving you like that? Anybody ever make that
kind of sacrifice for you? The following story shows, in a way, what Christ has
done for you.

> Around the turn of the century, a boy lived with his grandmother. One
> night his grandmother's house caught on fire, and she perished trying to
> get to the little boy upstairs. A crowd soon gathered to watch the specta-
> cle, and the boy's cries could be heard above the roaring blaze. Suddenly a
> stranger rushed from the crowd and went to the back of the house, where
> he spotted an iron pipe leading to the second floor. Hand over hand he
> climbed the hot pipe and reached an upstairs window. The man disap-
> peared for a minute, then climbed down the hot pipe with the boy tightly
> hanging on to his neck.
>
> Weeks later a public meeting was held in the town hall to determine
> custody of the boy. Each person who wanted the boy was permitted to
> speak briefly. The first man said, "I have a big farm. Every boy needs
> plenty of wide-open space to play." The second man stepped up and said,

"I'm a teacher. I have a large library. He would get a good education with me." Others came forward. Finally the richest man in town came up and said, "I'm wealthy. I could give the boy everything: farm, books, education, money, and even travel. I would like to have him live in our home."

The chairman asked, "Is there anyone else who would like to say a word?" Then in the back of the room a man stood up. As he walked forward, people could see deep suffering on his face. Once at the front of the room, he stood directly in front of the little boy. Slowly the stranger took his hands out of his pockets. A gasp went up from the crowd. The little boy, who had been staring at the floor the whole time, now looked up. The man's hands were terribly scarred. The boy cried out in recognition. Here was the man who had saved his life. The man's hands were burned from climbing up and down the hot pipe. No questions were needed. The boy threw his arms around the stranger's neck and held on for life.

The farmer got up and left. The teacher, too, and then the rich man. Everyone departed, leaving the boy alone with his rescuer, who had won custody of him without ever saying a word. Those scarred hands and the man's sacrifice spoke more powerfully than anything else.

Today, many things compete for your loyalty—friends, popularity, school, sports, job. But there is one who comes down through time, who, by merely raising his nail-pierced hands, reminds you of the incredible price he paid for you. He bought you with his own life.

Spend some time in prayer right now, meditating on John 3:16. Think about Jesus' sacrifice for you. Think about how much Jesus must love you to suffer and die for you in order to take your sin and God's wrath on himself. Thank God that he loved you enough to send his one and only Son to earth.

I need to remember that God loves me and sent his Son for me!

Keep It Simple

Rain Love

Ever wonder if some people have a little too much time on their hands? A study was done at a university in Utah in which cattle on the range were fitted with special breathing devices. Why? To study their burps. That's right. A half million dollars to study cow burps. The researchers wanted to see if the methane released from cow burps contributed to global warming. If the polar ice caps start to melt, you can blame ol' Bessie.

Do you ever wonder how some people focus on all the wrong things in life and miss what's really important? For example:

- Your mom complains about the one B you made and ignores the four A's.
- Pro athletes argue over multimillion-dollar contracts and forget about the sport.
- People go to church to worship but get upset about the color of the carpet.
- Your team beats the crosstown rival, but you're upset because it was by only one point.
- Somebody wins free tickets to the Super Bowl but complains about the seats.
- Your dad offers to buy you a new car, but it doesn't come in your favorite color.

At times we all manage to focus on all the wrong things. We forget what's really important. The same thing can be said about the Christian life. You can complicate your relationship with God, making it confusing and even frustrating because you're focusing on everything but the relationship itself.

It seems to be a law of life that we tend to complicate the simple things and end up missing the point altogether. Christians have had this problem for centuries. Turn to 2 Corinthians 11 and read verses 1-3.

How does Paul describe one's relationship with Christ? (v. 2)

What was his concern for the believers at Corinth? (v. 3)

Paul had introduced the Corinthians to Christ. He had promised or "engaged" them to him. As a result, Paul cared very deeply about their relationship with Christ, but he feared that other things might get in the way of that relationship and turn their focus away from what was really important.

What example does he use in verse 3?

Think about Adam and Eve. God had provided everything they needed. All they had to do was enjoy what God had made for them. They walked with God and talked with him. It was just them and God. They had only one simple thing to avoid. Life wasn't very complicated. But Satan wanted them to think they needed more than what God had said. He wanted them to add something else to their lives—the knowledge of good and evil. God's plan was to keep it simple and obey him. But they chose to disobey God and complicate matters and clutter up their relationship with God. Sin ended up making a huge mess. Like Christmas lights tangled up in knots, Adam and Eve's relationship with God became very chaotic and complex.

What gets in the way of your relationship with Jesus?

Look over this list and mark off the stuff you don't think is absolutely necessary in your relationship with Christ. In other words, what could you do without?

- The Bible
- Church
- Christian books
- Christian T-shirts
- Preaching

- Prayer
- Fellowship
- Youth trips
- Fun/Entertainment
- Music

None of these things is bad, but some stuff clutters your relationship with Christ. What does a simple and pure devotion look like?

> Take Dave and Julie. They're engaged to be married. They aren't worried about how much money they have. Julie doesn't care what kind of car Dave drives. They don't care about what might happen in the future. They're in love and can't wait to be together. They think about each other day and night. They dream about being together. Sometimes they are unaware that anyone else even exists! They're in love! That's simple and pure devotion.

What are some ways you can simplify your relationship with Christ?

I need to keep my relationship with Christ simple and clutter-free.

Worship Basics

R a i n   L o v e

Local residents say he is a god. They wear plastic badges over their hearts and hang his picture in their homes, offices, restaurants, and subways. Each day, people wipe their pictures, keeping them free from dust. At school, children march in rank, chanting allegiance to him. On national television, people wail and weep before a sixty-six-foot bronze statue of his likeness. Thousands of small children cry when his name is mentioned. Who is this person? He is Kim Il Sung, the late ruler of North Korea. After ruling that country for decades, Sung died and left his power to his son, who is also worshiped as a god.

Why would an entire nation worship a ruler like this? According to his followers, there was no problem he could not solve. He had done so much for the country. They believe he was an expert on virtually everything. They believe he is a god, and they worship him.

All around the world, people worship everything from the sun, moon, and stars to the mountains and rivers to dead ancestors to religious figures, past and present. But as Christians, we must worship only one person. Remember the first of the Ten Commandments?

Do not worship any other gods besides me. (Exodus 20:3)

But what does worship look like? When you think of God's great love that he has rained down on you, how are you supposed to respond? Is worship standing at attention or singing hymns on Sunday morning? Is it putting money in an offering plate? Is it thinking about God in prayer? Is it lifting your hands? Is it jumping up and down at a Christian concert? Just what is worship and how do you do it?

What is worship to you? What helps you worship God? Look at this list and write *yes* or *no* beside each item, indicating whether or not it helps you worship God.

- Organ music ____
- Hymns ____
- Standing up ____
- Choruses ____
- Lifting your hands ____
- Being alone ____
- Being in a large crowd ____

- Contemporary music ____
- Being quiet ____
- Being indoors ____
- Writing down your thoughts ____
- Being outdoors ____
- Praying outloud ____

There are many different ways to express worship, but they still don't explain what worship is. The word *worship* comes from two words—*worth* and *ship*. It literally means to describe the worth of something or someone.

Look up Revelation 5:9. How is Jesus described in this verse?

Why is he worthy?

Look down at verse 12. Because Jesus is worthy, what does he deserve?

Jot down a few words about what you think it means to
- glorify God
- honor God
- praise God

These are words we throw around a lot at church and in Christian circles. But we need to, in a sense, take them out of church and put them into our Monday—

Saturday lives too, don't we? We need to see worship as something we do together with other Christians at church as well as something we do at home, at school, after school, at work, with our friends, on Friday nights, and when we're alone.

What's one way you can tell God—with your life, not your lips—how worthy he is?

True worship is living out your praise to God through your actions. It is simply obeying God. You bring honor and glory to God every time you do what he wants you to do. The worship service doesn't end at 11:00 on Sunday. It continues throughout the week. Of course, you can't worship a God you don't know; that's why Bible study is so important. Through your time with God in his Word, you learn more about who he is. And the more you know him, the more you know how worthy he is to be worshiped. That's what Jesus meant when he said that "true worshipers" are those who worship "in spirit and in truth" (John 4:23).

We can learn a lot about devotion and loyalty from a dog named King.

King was a collie owned by a little boy—Angelo Del Plato. One day, Angelo was tragically killed in an accident. At the funeral, King stood on the outskirts of the crowd, and when the casket was being lowered into the ground, the faithful dog watched in disbelief, wondering how his master really could be gone. Soon after the funeral, King began the several-mile trip to his master's grave, each day lying down near the headstone for a while, then trotting back home. This continued every day for more than eight years! Even when tied up, King would manage to chew through the ropes and pull down posts to make it to the grave. Newspapers all over the country ran this amazing story of devotion and loyalty. Somehow, this loving dog had found a way to remain close to his master, even in death!

In a sense, your Master (Jesus) has gone. Christ no longer lives on earth in a human body. He is in heaven. The way you can worship him is not by going to his grave—he's not there—but by your loyal devotion and worship through the way you live for him and treat others.

TAKE-AWAY THOUGHT

I can worship God by living a life that brings honor to him.

CHAPTER TWO

Who'll Pray for Me?

I've been waiting for someone to notice
That I'm hurting. Who will pray for me?
It's so lonely in this silence. Can you pray for me?
If I'd ask you, would you pray for me?

Chorus:
Who'll pray for me
Who'll lift me up and set me free
Who'll stand by me
Who'll pray for me?

I'm walking yet there's no one standing by me.
The changing in this world could use some change.
So desperate if they find out, they will fear me.
If they judge me, who'll pray for me?

[repeat chorus]

Chorus 2:
Who'll face the cross upon their knees
Who'll stand by me
Who'll pray for me?

A real friend is the one thing that I'm needing—
Someone who already understands.
Still I'm searching for the answer and forgiveness.
If you're out there, would you pray for me?

"Who'll Pray for Me"
Words and Music by Al Denson, Robert White Johnson, and Chris Pelcer
© 1997 Paragon Music Corp. / ASCAP / RadioQuest Music Publishing
/ BMI / Million Suns Music / BMI / Al Denson Music / ASCAP.

Solve the Mystery of Prayer DAY 4

Who'll Pray for Me?

> amie said, "I bet you don't even know the Lord's Prayer."
>
> "Of course I do," Kevin shot back.
>
> "Ten dollars says you don't," said Jamie.
>
> "That's easy," Kevin replied and then began: "Now I lay me down to sleep; I pray the Lord my soul to keep."
>
> Jamie looked at him in amazement. "Wow, Kevin! I really didn't think you could do it!"

Most people can rattle off the Lord's Prayer. (The real prayer can be found in Matthew 6:9-13.) But how much do we really know about prayer itself?

What would you say most people your age think prayer is?

- Something you do in church
- Something you do before a meal
- Something you do in an emergency
- Something you do when you're outdoors around nature
- Something only holy people do—like preachers, priests, and grandmothers
- Something everyone *ought* to do, but not many people *really* do
- Something you do at special times of the year—like Christmas and Easter

There are a lot of misconceptions out there about prayer, and there are also lots of questions you might have about prayer, such as:

- What is prayer?
- How am I supposed to do it—when, where, how long?
- How can I pray so that God will listen?
- How can I pray for other people?
- Is it wrong to pray for certain things?
- Should I pray out loud or silently?
- What about praying in public?
- What does it mean to pray "in Jesus' name"?
- What if God doesn't answer me?
- How can I be consistent in praying?

During the next few days, you're going to discover answers to many of those questions. But most important, you're going to actually spend time praying to your heavenly Father.

Let's begin by answering two basic questions about prayer.

What's the purpose of prayer?

Look up the following verse and see if you can come up with a definition of prayer.

Exodus 33:11

Prayer is _____

You could say that the Bible is one way God talks to you, and prayer is your way of talking with God. Like a child talking to his father, or a friend talking to a friend, prayer is telling God your thoughts, needs, and feelings. If that's true, you shouldn't be afraid to pray.

What should I say in prayer?

You can talk to God about anything you want—absolutely anything. When Jesus' disciples asked him to teach them to pray, he gave them a model to follow. This prayer (the Lord's Prayer) is not meant to be a ritual or a rigid structure, but rather it gives us an example of the kind of prayer that will deepen our relationship with God.

Read Matthew 6:9-13.

Based on the Lord's Prayer, we discover four parts that are basic to any prayer:

- *Adoration—"Hallowed be thy name"*

    This is the same as praise. In other words, let God know how awesome you think he is.

    What is one thing about God you think is awesome?

- *Submission—"Thy will be done"*

    This means giving God total control of your life and obeying his plans instead of going your own way.

    What area of your life do you still need to place under his control?

- *Petition—"Give us this day our daily bread"*

    Petitioning God means asking God to meet your needs. Petition also includes praying for other people's needs. Prayer requests belong under the petition category.

    What is one of your prayer requests today?

- *Confession—"Forgive us"*

    Confession of your sins is extremely important to your relationship with God.

    What sins do you need to confess?

In a nutshell, that is what prayer is all about.

End this study in prayer, using these basic elements. Go through each phrase and put it in your own words. For example: "Our Father, who art in heaven, hallowed be thy name" could be "Heavenly Father, you're awesome because you are all-powerful," and so on.

TAKE-AWAY THOUGHT **Prayer is talking to God and having fellowship with him.**

Anytime at All

Who'll Pray for Me?

I told him to call me anytime he needed me, but I never really expected him to take me seriously. Brad (not his real name) was struggling with drug addiction. In an effort to help, I had agreed to meet with him once a week to study the Bible, pray, and just be a friend to him. Brad was a great guy with a big heart, and I genuinely liked him. I truly believed that God was going to bring him out of his addiction and put him back on the road to wellness—physically and spiritually. After almost a year of meeting together, we were seeing some real progress.

It was December 23. I was out of school for the holidays and was looking forward to spending a lot of time at home. Late that night the phone rang. It was Brad. He had been kicked out of his house and had fallen back into some of his old habits. It was a cold night, and he was at a pay phone. "Can you help me?" Brad pleaded. "I need to talk to you. Can you come and pick me up?" At first I didn't want to go. I was hanging out at home, warm, comfortable. To be honest, it kind of bothered me to be called late at night. Like I said, when I told him to "call me anytime," I never thought he would actually take me up on it. But those were my words, and I had to stick by them. Bundling up, I climbed into my Jeep and headed out to help Brad.

I learned some valuable lessons from that experience with Brad. I learned that life is not always convenient. I also learned that anytime at all meant anytime at all! Fortunately, God is not like me (or you, for that matter). He is not bothered when we call on him, even in the middle of the night. There are no inconvenient times to him. He is never too busy to talk to us or help us. He's available twenty-four hours a day.

Today, you will learn what a privilege it is to come to God in prayer for anything in your life. This is called access to God through prayer.

Find Hebrews 4 and read verses 15-16.

What do you learn about Jesus from verse 15?

Because of this, what can you do with confidence? Why? (v. 16)

Do you feel you can go to God anytime?

Are there times when you don't feel comfortable or good enough to go to him?

What do you discover in these verses that might help you during those times?

If you look back on the life of Christ, you'll recall that Jesus never refused anyone who came to him.

Jesus accepted all of them, and he'll accept and welcome you into his presence. Remember, in John 6:37, Jesus promised:

> Those the Father has given me will come to me, and I will never reject them.

Because of what Jesus did through his death on the cross—paying your sin debt in full—you can now have complete and unrestricted access to him. You can enter into the very presence of the one who spoke the universe into existence—24 hours a day, 7 days a week, 365 days a year—anytime at all!

God is there when you need him, when you feel far away from him, when a friend lets you down, when you sin, when your family is falling apart, when your day has been a total disaster, when you're facing a big decision or a huge problem, when you need direction, when your future is uncertain, when you're weak, when you're alone, when your burden is too big to carry, when you just can't go on. Prayer is there. God is there. Go to him.

Write out a prayer right now to the Lord, thanking him for the unlimited access you have into his presence because of what he did for you on the cross.

Because of Jesus, I can go to God in prayer anytime.

Keep the Line Open
Who'll Pray for Me?

Chris and Angie had been dating for three months, and they were starting to get pretty serious. They spent nearly every day after school over at Angie's house, studying together. Then they would spend hours on the phone talking to each other. One night, while on the phone, Chris finally got up the nerve and decided he would ask Angie to go steady with him. This was a big deal to him, since he had never done that before. Because he was so nervous, he wrote out what he wanted to say.

"Angie, I've been thinking about this for a while, and I want you to know that I don't want to go out with any other girl from now on. You are the only girl I love and I'm not interested in anyone else but you. Please go steady with me. I'm going away soon on vacation so I need an answer now."

Unfortunately for Chris, the phone company had been working on the lines in his area, making the connection between him and Angie distorted and hard to understand. What Angela actually heard was:

"Angie, I've been thinking about this for a while, and I . . . don't want to go out . . . from now on. You are the only girl . . . I'm not interested in . . . Please go . . . away soon . . . now."

The last thing Chris heard was a dial tone.

Can you say "bad connection"?

It's hard to carry on a conversation with someone when you don't get through to them or they can't correctly hear what you're saying. The same is true in your relationship with God. As we continue to think about prayer as a conversation with our heavenly Father, there are some things that create a bad connection and block our prayers.

Take heart, though. God understands this problem. He has told us in his Word what these obstacles to prayer are and how we can get rid of them. From the following verses, see if you can find out what disconnects our prayers from God and how you can reconnect.

Disconnection 1 _____ (Psalm 66:18)

Like a barrier, sin comes between you and God. The line goes dead. It's like you're calling heaven and you keep getting a dial tone. Find the following verses and jot down what Jesus says about sin and our prayers.

- Luke 18:10-14

- Mark 11:25

Solution to a clear line _____ (Psalm 32:5)

Disconnection 2—Praying in order to _____(Matthew 6:5)

A little four-year-old was saying his prayers with his mom one night before going to bed. When he began whispering, his mother interrupted, "Sweetheart, speak up. Mommy can't hear you."
"But, Mom," the boy protested, "I wasn't talking to you."

Too often when we pray with others, we end up praying in a way we think sounds good to them. We forget that in group prayer, we are still praying our own heart to God. We're just letting other people listen in on the conversation. We can even try to impress ourselves when we're alone by using religious language and words that sound spiritual but don't really come from our heart.

Solution to a clear line _____ (Matthew 6:6)

Disconnection 3—Praying with _____ motives (James 4:3)

If we're not careful, our prayers can end up centering around three people—me, myself, and I. It's a one-sided conversation with ourselves as the focus. Though we are to pray about our own needs and wants, we must be careful that we don't become the main attraction in our prayers.

Solution to a clear line _____ (James 4:7-8)

How about a little prayer inventory? If you were to evaluate your prayer life, what percentage of your time in prayer would you say involves:

Praise and adoration?   _____
Confession?   _____
Praying for yourself?   _____
Praying for others?   _____
Your mind wandering?   _____
Total   _____

(Remember, it should add up to 100 percent.)

Which one of the three major disconnections do you struggle with the most?

　　1—Unconfessed sin

　　2—Praying in order to impress others

　　3—Praying with selfish motives

What do you think you can do to keep this obstacle out of your prayer life?

TAKE-AWAY THOUGHT

To communicate with God, I must maintain a clear connection in prayer.

If you could give a gift to the president of the United States, what would it be? Well, back in the summer of 1801, a group of men, spearheaded by a Baptist minister named John Leland, got together to decide what gift they would give to their president, Thomas Jefferson. A decision was made, and Pastor Leland's congregation went out and milked 900 cows at the same time, then produced a hunk of cheese 4 feet wide and 15 inches thick, weighing 1,235 pounds! The colossal chunk of cheese was then delivered to the White House on New Year's Day, 1802, in a cart pulled by a team of six horses bearing a sign which read, The Greatest Cheese in America for the Greatest Man in America.

President Jefferson paid the gift givers two hundred dollars for their labor of love. And what became of the cheese? Historians record that the White House ate from that hunk of cheese for the next three years!

When you think of cheesy things to do for a person, that certainly rates right up there at the top. But seriously, when you think of giving gifts or doing something special for friends, what comes to mind? Write some of the best gifts you've ever given.

- hanging out with them
- writing a letter to them
- taking class notes for them
- buying them a new CD
- _____
- _____

One of the things that makes a gift meaningful is its appropriateness. And nothing could be more appropriate than giving the gift of prayer. That's right. Praying for someone can do more for him or her than money or material gifts (or cheese!) ever could. To be honest, it often sounds trivial to say to someone, "I'll be praying for you," doesn't it? It sounds too ordinary to just pray.

Why do you suppose we sometimes view prayer this way?

Why does God say we ought to pray for one another? (James 5:16)

What is another reason to pray for a friend? (Galatians 6:2)

We should pray for our friends whenever they have needs:

- physical needs—they're sick or in pain
- emotional needs—they're depressed or hurting
- spiritual needs—they need salvation or help in their walk with God
- social needs—they feel lonely or need a friend
- financial needs—they need money

Of course, if you can help meet any of these needs, then you should do so. Prayer demonstrates your love and concern for your friends. It is all about support. It's going to the King on behalf of someone else, asking for help for them.

How do you pray for someone else? Just talk to God as you would any other time. Tell him what you think and feel. Don't be afraid to ask him for big things, either. You might want to model your prayers after the apostle Paul as he prayed for his friends. Here are some of Paul's well-known prayers for other Christians:

- Philippians 1:9-11
- Colossians 1:9-14
- 1 Thessalonians 3:9-13

Back in the Old Testament, God, through his prophet Ezekiel, called out to the nation of Israel. Spiritually, times were bad. It seemed as if every man was out for himself. It was at this time God spoke through Ezekiel to the people, saying, "I looked for someone who might rebuild the wall of righteousness that guards the land. I searched for someone to stand in the gap in the wall so I wouldn't have to destroy the land, but I found no one" (Ezekiel 22:30). God still wants people who will "stand in the gap" between him and man through prayer. Will you begin to pray regularly for others? Think about forming a small prayer group of three or four friends—just to pray together once a week.

Are there any family members or friends who need prayer? Write down their names, and spend some time right now standing in the gap for them through prayer.

- Do any of your friends need to trust Christ as Savior?
- Do any of your friends need to get back together with God?
- Who has emotional needs?
- Who has physical needs?
- Are any of your friends having family problems?

Mike had stopped for a red light in a downtown district of a big city. A homeless man approached his car and tapped on the window. "Can I have something for my box, mister?" the man asked. Mike replied, "Sorry, I don't have any money." Mike began rolling up his window. The crazy said, "My name's Howard. What's yours?"

"Mike," he said. Stooping down, the man picked up a scrap of paper from the sidewalk, took out a broken pencil, and began scribbling something down. Just then the light changed, and Mike took off.

A few days later, as he drove through the same area, Mike noticed an ambulance parked outside an alley. Pulling over, he got out and joined the other curious onlookers. Two paramedics came out of the alley carrying a stretcher. It was "Howard the crazy." As they loaded him into the ambulance, a policeman began questioning the crowd to see if anyone had any information about the homeless man.

Finally Mike spoke up. "His name is Howard. That's all I know about him . . . just his name," Mike assured the policeman. The policeman picked up a box and gave it to Mike. "This is all he had. He won't be needing it anymore."

Feeling awkward and curious at the same time, Mike slowly opened the box. Inside, there was nothing but a few old clothes and a file folder. Printed across the top was the word *FRIENDS*. He opened it and looked inside. There was only one small scrap of paper. On it was written *Mike*.

You never know, do you? You may be the only true friend someone will ever have. You never know whose life you might help if you'll just reach out and simply be their friend. And one way you can do that is to pray for that person.

Will you pray?

TAKE-AWAY THOUGHT **One of the greatest things I can do for someone else is to faithfully pray for him or her.**

CHAPTER THREE

Right About Now

The truth's covered up with lies
It's hard to believe your eyes
When faith and love are nowhere left in sight
It's a crime they can never sell
And the press don't always tell
They justify the stories they create

No one can deny the fact there's a God
The evidence demands a verdict

Chorus:
Right about now
Things have got to change
It's a world going up in flames
High up on a cross
He was looking down
Wonderin' if we'd ever come around
Right about now

There's a child out in no-man's-land
With a pain no one understands
Will the shadow of darkness forever seal his fate?
It's a red light that we can't run
As we rise to a fading sun
Our days were numbered long before we knew

[repeat chorus]

Bridge:
Sure as we live and breathe
More than the love we need
The answer's so clear

[repeat chorus]

"Right About Now"
Words and Music by Al Denson, Robert White Johnson, and Chris Pelcer
© 1997 Paragon Music Corp. / ASCAP / RadioQuest Music Publishing
/ BMI / Million Suns Music / BMI / Al Denson Music / ASCAP.
All rights reserved. Used by permission.

X-Ray Vision DAY 8
Right About Now

Have you ever gone to the hospital ER? The X-ray technician takes an X-ray of your ankle, hands the doctor the film, and the doctor nods. Yeah, you broke your ankle. Your problem is treated. Case closed. You hobble out on crutches.

God wants to help you develop X-ray vision to see what others in your world cannot see. He wants you to be able to understand the true condition of human-kind and where this planet is headed. And seeing the truth about the world will certainly give you a clear perspective on life.

> **Harvey Weinstein knows what perspective is. The sixty-eight-year-old millionaire (he made his millions from selling tuxedoes) from New York City was kidnapped and buried in a hole in the ground for twelve days and nights. During that time, he fought insanity by remembering the things in his life that were important to him—all the way back to age six. In his isolation, he lost hope many times, thinking that no one would find him and that he would never see his family again. But after twelve days alone in the dark, Harvey felt the touch of a New York City detective reach down into that hole. He later recalled, "I knew God had smiled down on me." Harvey gained a little perspective during his stay in "Hell's Hole." He sees everything now in a different light.**

Living here on earth can sometimes feel like living in a dark hole. As you look around, it doesn't take much insight to see that things are rapidly deteriorating on this planet. It seems the human race is being drawn into a giant whirlpool of evil, spiraling downward into self-destruction.

How can we understand what's going on? Where does this special X-ray vision come from? It comes from your accurate understanding of the Bible. In it, God reveals to you what the world is really like and how you are to relate to it. Through Scripture, you have the special ability to see straight through the lies and philosophies bombarding you through TV, magazines, and movies.

So open your Bible and prepare to see for yourself!

Look up 1 John 2:17. What does God say about this world?

You might remember that God totally destroyed the world once before (2 Peter 3:5-6). According to 2 Peter 3:10, how is God going to bring the world to its final end?

Does the average person at your school really believe this is going to happen? If not, what do you think *they* would say is the future of human-kind and the planet? (Keep in mind that they may only see the surface. They might not have spiritual X-ray vision.)

After reading 2 Peter 3:11-12, complete this sentence: Knowing these things about the world should cause me to

The year was 1912, and all of Britain was buzzing with talk of their latest achievement—a British steamship—the largest ship ever built. Measuring 882 feet and weighing over 46,000 tons, the *Titanic* was billed as the "Eighth Wonder of the World."

Sailing from Southampton, the massive vessel began her maiden voyage to New York with twenty-two hundred passengers aboard. As the colossal ocean liner cut its way across the chilly North Atlantic, not a soul on board had any idea of the catastrophe that was about to occur. This was a floating city. Gigantic. Unsinkable. In fact, *Titanic's* builders claimed that "God himself couldn't sink her."

Somebody forgot to tell God that.

On April 14, shortly before midnight, the *Titanic* struck a huge iceberg, ripping open a three-hundred-foot gash in her side. Immediately, water began gushing into her hull. Still believing that the ship could not sink, many passengers didn't even try to get on a lifeboat for some time, When they finally began clamoring for lifeboats, panic soon became widespread. It became clear that there were not enough lifeboats for all the passengers. Husbands said hurried, tearful good-byes to their wives and children. Families were separated as hundreds climbed over each other, scrambling to safety. Panicked passengers jumped overboard only to freeze or drown in the deep, icy waters of the Atlantic or to be sucked underwater by the immense whirlpool created by the sinking liner. Others were trapped in the lower decks, unable to go up to where the lifeboats were.

All in all, 1,513 lives were lost. Today, the sinking of the *Titanic* is regarded as one of the greatest human disasters of the twentieth century.

Friend, this world is the *Titanic*. Proudly sailing along and ignoring constant warnings from heaven, the world has struck a massive iceberg of sin—a reality people love to deny. And the "not so good" ship *Earth* is rapidly taking on the waters of God's judgment. Some still believe it cannot sink. "Everything will be OK," they say. "We can take on water and still stay afloat." But the grim reality is that God says the world is going down, or rather, up in flames. The question is, where will you end up—on the sinking ship of this world or in the lifeboat of God's will? Will you let friends on board drag you down to the bottom with them? Or will you get on board with God completely?

One thing is for sure—it is impossible to have one foot on the *Titanic* and one foot in the lifeboat. It's one or the other, but not both.

So what's your mind-set? Where will your loyalty be? Where will your devotion be today?

Understanding what God says about the future of the world will help me live for him in the present.

Take a Stand DAY 9
Right About Now

Imagine you lived in a country that did not allow freedom of religion. There are no churches in this country. No Bibles. No prayer groups. No "See You at the Pole" gatherings. No campus ministries. No youth groups. No Bible studies. No Christian music. No Christian radio and no Al Denson concerts (gasp!). In fact, it is against the law there to worship the God of the Bible in any way. It is literally a godless land. How strong do you think your faith would be? Would your devotion to God thrive, barely survive, or die?

Well, there's a manual on how to thrive in a godless land. In the third chapter of the book of Daniel, we read about three teenaged boys who lived in just such a country. Their identity was taken away—their homes, their families, their country, their culture, their customs—all gone. Even their names were changed to fit their new country. As far as they were concerned, it was the end of their world. There was nothing left.

Nothing except their faith, that is.

And that's all the three needed. You see, these teenagers were godly young men, fiercely committed to the Lord. Their real names were Hananiah, Mishael and Azariah—but we know them better as Shadrach, Meshach, and Abednego. These Hebrew teenagers kept their faith in God in a pagan world (much like ours) even when it meant paying a great price. But through their courageous story, we uncover some incredible principles about how we can stand strong just as they did.

This is their story.

Begin by reading Daniel 3:1-6.

What pressure did the three young men confront?

What was the penalty for not going along with the crowd?

(No fines. No running laps. No D-Hall. No demerits. No suspension. No expulsion—just instant death!)

How did the king find out that these Hebrew boys refused to bow down to the idol? (3:7-12)

Imagine the scene. Thousands of people in this emperor-worshiping mob hit the deck every time they heard the music play. These people lived to please the king. They never dreamed of not bowing down. Besides, everybody was doing it. It never occurred to them that someone would be foolish enough to disobey the king. Only a fool would go against the law of the land. Who would want to risk public humiliation and social embarrassment, not to mention their lives? So why not go along? Give up. Give in. Obey. Bow.

So thousands of people bowed down—everybody except for Shadrach, Meshach, and Abednego. They probably locked their knees tight and stood tall. Think of how they must have stood out. Think of the stares. The whispers. The jeers. The ridicule. They were about to become the laughingstock of the city.

This wasn't about "saying no" to drugs or not drinking at a party. They weren't standing for Jesus by putting a Christian bumper sticker on their car or wearing a

Christian T-shirt to school. This was a spiritual showdown on Main Street, Babylon—the mightiest nation on earth at that time. It was a winner-take-all match between an evil world and three godly teenagers. It was external pressure versus internal devotion. By doing nothing but standing, these boys single-handedly took on the king and his godless decree. By standing their ground, they won.

He shoots, he scores!

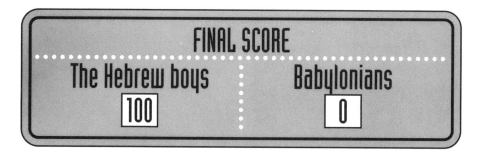

How could they do that? Because the three young men feared God more than they feared Nebuchadnezzar. They respected the King of heaven more than a king on earth. They lived to please God and God alone.

It all boiled down to this one question: Whose approval are we seeking—God's or the world's? Shadrach, Meshach, and Abednego had already made up their minds. They knew this world wouldn't last forever, and neither would its kings or their kingdoms. But God would still be there. Better to obey him, and so they stood—no matter what the consequences (that's tomorrow's story).

So how does the pressure they faced relate to your life today? That was then, this is now, right? Right. But some things never change. For example, in what ways is the world still trying to pressure you into "bowing down" to its demands? How does the world expect you to immediately conform to its standards in these areas:

- Friendships
- Money
- Music
- Relationship with parents

In what other ways does the world attempt to squeeze you into its mold?

Is there anything in the example of these three that you could follow for your life?

TAKE-AWAY THOUGHT **Pleasing God has to be my highest priority.**

The Price Tag of Commitment

Right About Now

Shelly's principal told her that she could not start a Christian club on her high school campus. Discouraged but persistent, she asked if she and her Christian friends could just meet to pray together. She was emphatically told, "There will be no prayer on this campus." But Shelly wouldn't give up, even when she was harassed in the hallways by teachers. She was even called in for a special meeting with the school-district superintendent. But Shelly persisted and prayed.

Because of her uncompromising stand, word soon spread on campus, and she was branded as a fanatic by her classmates. Nevertheless, she stood strong in her commitment. Finally, after some gentle persuasion from a Christian attorney, the school allowed a prayer group to meet every Wednesday morning at seven-thirty. And the club? At the first meeting over seventy students packed into the small classroom that they used as a meeting room. That club continues to meet today. And it all happened because one girl had the faith to believe. That's courageous faith!

An old preacher once said, "The Christian life that costs nothing accomplishes nothing." If you really want your life to count on this planet, you may have to pay a price. It's called sacrifice. Great athletes know all about sacrifice. So do accomplished musicians. They dedicate themselves each day to grueling hours of practice and training.

Nowadays, many Christians want all the benefits of the Christian life but none of the sacrifices that come with it. While salvation is totally free, living for

God costs us everything we have. The reality of the Christian life is that there are both blessings *and* hardships. We have to take the joys with the sorrows. The victory of Easter only came after the pain of Good Friday. If you stand up for Jesus Christ, you will become a lightning rod, deflecting strikes from the enemy. Like Shelly.

Maybe you can identify with her. Perhaps you've taken some heat because of your dedication to God. Maybe you've caught flak from your classmates for your Christian lifestyle. If so, then take heart, because you're not alone. You're in good company. There are those three teenaged boys who know exactly how you feel.

Let's read the rest of the story of Shadrach and his friends.

> Looking at Daniel 3:13-15, how did King Nebuchadnezzar react when he heard that these three boys had refused to bow down?

He was furious, claiming that there was no god who could deliver them out of the king's hands. Look up the word *overconfidence* in a dictionary and you might see Nebuchadnezzar's picture there. However, because of the king's fondness for the boys, he does at least give them a chance to respond and change their minds.

> But according to verses 16-18, why didn't they change their minds?

Now imagine what they *could* have done. They could have called a time-out and formed a huddle to brainstorm ways to get out of their predicament. They could have said:

- Hello! If we're dead, God can't use us then! Death isn't in our contract!
- What are we doing here? The king likes us. We can't let him down.
- Our promotion and advancement in the kingdom depend on obeying him.

- Idols aren't real anyway. So what harm could it do?
- We'll just do it once, then we'll confess it.
- Everyone else is doing it.
- We'll bow, but in our hearts we'll be praying to God.
- Doing this will help us reach more people because they'll see that we're like them.

That's what they *could* have said. Instead, there wasn't even a discussion. No time-out. No thinking it over. No compromise. This was a no-brainer for them. They stood firm together. Like huge stone boulders of confidence, they weren't about to budge an inch. It was external pressure against inward devotion. Besides, they knew their God was all-powerful and would be with them—even in death. They were living for the eternal world to come, not for the temporary world around them.

In what ways does this happen to you today?

- It happens when your coach says you can't stay on the team if you keep missing practice because of youth group.
- It happens when your boss says you have to work on Sundays or you will be fired. And no job means no gas money, no spending money, no car payment, no new CDs, no nothing!
- It happens every time you are excluded from a group because of what you believe or what you refuse to do.

But think of the enormous pressure these three guys were under. What do you think you would have done if you were with these guys?

Knowing me, I would have

hit the deck

passed out

burst into tears

made a run for it

argued with the king

tried to strike a compromise

stood with no fear

stood but would have been afraid (which would have been OK in God's eyes)

The three could stand because of their conviction and commitment. They were in it together and knew God was on their side.

TAKE-AWAY THOUGHT When my beliefs cost me, I can stand strong with other Christians and with God on my side.

"Fired Up" for God

Right About Now

The Wright brothers. John Glenn. Christopher Columbus. Neil Armstrong. Sir Edmund Hillary. Chuck Yeager. What do all these people have in common? They are all part of an elite "fraternity of firsts." Each of them was the first to accomplish something great in his area of exploration or adventure. From Mount Everest to the moon, each of these men enjoys a sense of immortality because of his amazing feats and accomplishments. But do you know who was the first Christian to die for his faith in Jesus? His name was Stephen. After he preached a sermon (recorded in Acts 7), his audience became angry, dragged him out of the city, and stoned him to death. Stoning in those days was a slow and painful death. The person being stoned was pelted with rocks from all sides that caused deep cuts, bruises, fractures, profuse bleeding, and eventually death. That's what happened to Stephen. As his stoning went on, Stephen lifted his eyes toward heaven and saw Jesus standing there to welcome him home. Amazingly, in spite of terrific pain and suffering, Stephen had peace knowing Jesus was there waiting for him. Stephen even asked Jesus not to hold this sin against the people (see Acts 7:60).

Shadrach, Meshach, and Abednego probably felt that same kind of peace. They were about to die, yet somehow they had this incredible peace. Their decision not to bow to Nebuchadnezzar's statue didn't exactly earn them brownie points with the king. In fact, these guys were probably voted "Most Likely to Burn" by the royal family that year. The king exploded in anger and heated up the furnace seven times hotter than normal, a decision he would later regret (see Daniel 3:19-22). These three amigos were then tied up and thrown into the furnace. End of story. Right?

Nope. Something in the fire caught the king's attention.

What was it? (Daniel 3:24-25)

How does Nebuchadnezzar describe this person?

Who do you think it was? (Check out Hebrews 13:5.)

Notice that Shadrach and his friends weren't looking for an exit door. They weren't trying to find a way out of suffering for God. The presence of God comforted them, and it convinced everyone else that their God was the one true God.

What does God promise you when you "go through the fire" for him? (Read Isaiah 43:1-2.)

How does knowing this make you feel?

What did the king do as a result of seeing all this? (vv. 26-27)

In verse 28, Nebuchadnezzar expressed his awe for this kind of God who could get this kind of all-or-nothing loyalty. He then honored both God and the three teenagers (vv. 29-30). They even got promotions!

Slim chance you'll get a standing ovation for sticking to your principles at the next pep rally. In fact, persecution may continue or even increase. But remember, you don't exist to please the world. As long as you live to please God, his presence will see you through the fire. He will honor you.

These three teenagers knew that. That's because they took God at his word. They were convinced that God kept his promises. They also knew who they were.

The royal court knew them by their Babylonian names. However, their true identities were revealed in the meanings of their Hebrew names.

- The Babylonian name Shadrach means "Exalt Aku."
- The Hebrew name Hananiah means "The Lord is gracious."
- The Babylonian name Meshach means "Who is what Aku is?"
- The Hebrew name Mishael means "Who is what the Lord is?"
- The Babylonian name Abednego means "The servant of Nebo."
- The Hebrew name Azariah means "The Lord is my Helper."

Close by praying this prayer to the Lord.
God,

I know you are looking for people who don't fear external pressure. I want to be that kind of person. I know you are searching for people who know who they're living for. I want to be that kind of person. I know you are seeking teenagers who will stand up even when everybody else is bowing down. I want to be that kind of teenager. Lord, help me to be all you want me to be and to have the courage to stand for my convictions. I know you are worthy of this kind of dedication and loyalty, so I gladly represent you to my world today.

For Jesus' sake,
Your loving child

When I stand for Christ, he stands with me.

CHAPTER FOUR

Fly with the Angels

When your life escapes you like a runaway train
And the place you come from is a state of pain
They can lift your spirits high above the pouring rain

The truth lies waiting in the sky above
You can sail forever in the presence of
Way up here you'll meet a great kind of love

Chorus:
You'll be flying with angels
Flying with angels
Flying with angels

On the wings of heaven you will carry love's flame
Like a voice of mercy you will hear your name
When the stones of life rock your world
You'll stake your claim

[repeat chorus]

Channel A:
Flyin', flyin', flyin' with angels
Flyin', flyin', flyin' with angels
Flyin', flyin', flyin' with angels

Channel B:
I know a place
It's yours if you believe
Through God's Son you'll see

Bridge:
There's peace up here in the open sky
You can see forever through angels' eyes

Headaches and Heartaches

Fly with the Angels

One of the most bizarre accidents in American history took place on September 13, 1847. A twenty-five-year-old railroad foreman named Phineas P. Gage was preparing a blast of dynamite when it unexpectedly exploded, driving a three-foot long, thirteen-pound iron bar through the left side of his face, continuing through his brain and out the back of his head (that'll leave a mark!). Though he was blown backward by the blast, Gage miraculously remained conscious and even alert as doctors examined him. For a while, he became delirious and lost sight in one eye, but after several months he was back at work. Phineas lived for some years after the accident, and he was studied by doctors from all over the country, who remained puzzled at how he could have survived. After his death, the iron bar, along with a cast of Gage's head, was placed in the museum of the Massachusetts Medical College.

One thing is sure. Nobody could ever say to Phineas Gage, "I know how you feel, man."

Your problems may not be as severe as poor old Phineas's, but you still face difficulties. In fact, there's not a person alive who doesn't battle with personal problems. You might even fight discouragement and depression. It's a part of life's curriculum. It's especially a part of the Christian life. Every believer in Christ faces trials, disappointments, and discouragement. They're like sharp arrows, dipped in the poison of despair, with your name written all over them. When these arrows of discouragement penetrate your heart, your spiritual tank dries up. It's easy to lose interest in spiritual things, and your desire for God begins to burn out. Resentment creeps in. You give up. You want to give in.

No matter what you face in life, there is usually someone who has experienced something the same or similar (unless, of course, you're Phineas Gage). And some of the people who can most identify with you are from the Bible. Just because they lived long ago doesn't mean their experiences weren't real and you can't learn from them. In fact, God put their stories in his Word so you could learn from them.

Take a look at 2 Corinthians 11:23-28. What are some of the trials Paul experienced?

Paul was well qualified to write on the subject of problems and trials. He faced some pretty tough trials and—let's be real—you will probably never suffer like Paul. One of Paul's disciples was a young man named Timothy. See if you can identify with what he was going through.

Look up 1 Timothy 4:12.

Describe the big struggles you think Timothy was facing.

Why would that be discouraging to someone?

What was Paul's advice to Timothy? (4:12)

Timothy also experienced many other problems in his church and in his personal life. In his second letter to Timothy, Paul refers to suffering, hardship, and trials more than ten times.

What problems have you faced this week?

Do you think anyone else has ever experienced the same things you're going through?

So what's the point? It's this—if you know these tough times are a normal part of life, it will keep you from freaking out when they come your way (James 1:2-3). Trials don't play favorites, but affect us all. Trials come in all shapes, sizes, and colors. We should not be surprised when they come into our lives. Imagine a football player being surprised because he got tackled. No way! He knows that getting tackled is part of the game. And he doesn't quit the game because he was tackled.

It's the same way with life. You aren't abnormal because you have problems. You're abnormal if you don't have them! So don't panic. Everybody goes through hard times. You're not alone.

TAKE-AWAY THOUGHT

Problems are part of life. I'm not alone, because all Christians go through struggles.

Tower of Power

Fly with the Angels

Y ears ago, I had a summer job as a groundskeeper. No, not at the country club, but at the local graveyard (don't laugh—I was young and I needed the money). It was a very large cemetery with a huge fence ('cause people were dying to get in!). I was only thirteen years old at the time, but I already felt grown-up. However, there was one thing that still frightened me—not ghosts and monsters, or even the dearly departed I mowed over—but thunder and lightning. For some reason, thunderstorms scared the life out of me. So, wouldn't you know it, one day right after lunch I'm mowing around a head-stone when I see this killer summer storm approaching. Before I could cut my mower off, the sky became dark, and thunder and lightning flashed all around me. I began to panic, looking around for a fresh hole to jump into (I scratched that plan in a hurry for fear I might bump into somebody down there!). Then I looked up and spotted the cemetery's huge bell tower about a hundred yards away in the middle of the cemetery.

By this time sheets of rain were pouring down, and the thunder was right on top of me. I took off like an Olympic sprinter, praying like mad that the tower door would be unlocked. In a matter of seconds I was there, and to my relief, it was unlocked. Yes! In that tower, over the sound of my own heartbeat, I could still hear the storm. But that was outside. I was inside. Safe. Protected. Secure. Insulated. Unafraid. I was one happy boy. Besides, I now had the rest of the day off.

Maybe when you were a little kid, you had a place like my bell tower. A place you could go when you were afraid. Perhaps it was under the covers in your bed, in your mom's or dad's lap, in a closet, or maybe in a secret hiding place. But what about now? Where is your "bell tower"? Where do you go when the storms of life are more than you can bear?

What place does Proverbs 18:10 describe?

What do you think it means to run to the Lord? How often do you do that?

How does David describe the Lord in Psalm 46:1?

What is a refuge? In what way is God a refuge to you?

What kind of help does God give?

Paul says the same thing when he encourages Timothy to "be strong with the special favor God gives you in Christ Jesus" (2 Timothy 2:1). This means to run to God's tower of strength and rest in his favor or grace. Think of how great it is just to relax sometimes. When do you relax and rest?

- after school?
- after a big game?
- after a monster test??
- after working in the yard?

- after cleaning your room?
- after visiting your relatives
- _____

It's just the opposite with God. Resting in him happens *before* you do something. He wants you to rest in *his* strength, not yours. That way you can always be strong. It's a simple law of life that the stronger you are, the more you can bear.

Once a little boy was trying to move a huge rock in his backyard. His father, noticing the boy's struggle, asked, "Son, aren't you using all your strength?"

"Of course I am, Dad," the young boy replied.

"But have you used all your power to move the rock?" the dad asked again.

"Dad, I'm pushing with everything I've got, but this big rock just won't budge!"

With that, the father came over to where the boy was, got down on his knees, looked his little boy in the eyes, and said, "Son, you haven't used all your strength until you ask your daddy to help you." And together, they easily moved the large rock.

It's the same with us. We haven't used all our strength to move our problem rocks until we ask our heavenly Father to help us. When we find our strength in him, we can handle anything (Philippians 4:13). The power is there. The strength is there. Just go to him, and rest in the safety of his arms.

Looking back over your relationship with God, do you think you treat God like a spiritual 911, running to him only in an emergency or crisis? Or is he more like a Father to you, to whom you run often to pour out your heart?

Do you really want the power to deal with the problems you face? If so, then you must be committed to trusting in God's strength to see you through each problem, one by one.

Why not run to him right now in prayer? Tell him everything you feel and everything that's bothering you.

When I face problems, I can run to the Lord for strength and safety.

When Life Doesn't Make Sense
Fly with the Angels

There are some things in life that are confusing to the average person. In fact, a lot of things don't add up. For example:

- Why are there interstate highways in Hawaii?
- How does the guy who drives the snowplow get to work in the mornings?
- If a cow laughed, would milk come out her nose?
- When we're driving and looking for an address, why do we turn down the volume on the radio?
- Why do we drive on parkways and park on driveways?
- Why is something that's transported by car called a "shipment," but when you transport something by ship, it's called "cargo"?

Why ask why?

On a more serious note, life really doesn't make a whole lot of sense at times. It can be downright confusing. Like putting a puzzle together without the picture to guide you, life can be frustrating and difficult to understand.

For example:

- Why does a sweet thirteen-year-old girl get a brain hemorrhage?
- Why does a senior in high school come down with cancer?
- Why do horrible things happen to good people while bad people seem to get away with all sorts of evil?

- Why do people who were once madly in love with one another get a divorce?
- Why are some children born with physical defects?
- Why can't adults understand teenagers?
- Why doesn't the person you really like, like you back?
- Why are some people cruel and unkind for no apparent reason?

> Does anybody really understand life in those times? I know I sure didn't. Two of my friends and I were flying from Dallas to San Antonio in a small plane. We had ten minutes left before landing. All three of us were pilots, but I wasn't the one flying the plane that day. None of us was prepared for what was about to happen. Suddenly, we developed engine trouble. Looking me straight in the eyes, my friend informed me that in forty-five seconds we were going to crash into the ground. As I braced myself, I began to think about actually seeing Jesus Christ in just a matter of seconds! Shortly after that, our plane smashed into the ground just outside San Antonio.
>
> Waking up in the hospital, I discovered I had suffered a broken leg, a broken arm, cuts, bruises, and I had 580 stitches in my face. My other friend had survived with minor injuries, but the pilot had died in the crash. Several thoughts kept echoing in my mind. *Why did this happen? Why did my friend die and I didn't? God, I just don't understand!*

Answers seem far away in times of crisis. It's one thing for someone else to go through those traumas, but it's another thing when the confusion happens to you! That's when life gets personal.

What should you do when the maze of life becomes more than you can handle? One thing you shouldn't do is face those times by yourself, because the problems only seem to get worse. It's easy during those times to become a spiritual loner, drifting away from God. You end up saying things you don't mean and doing things you later regret. That's why you shouldn't ever keep the pain to yourself. You need to have a friend or two with whom you can share your heart, someone you can be real with, somebody you can be yourself around. Good friends can relieve the stress and prevent you from blowing up (or shutting down!). God knows this. That's why he has put people in your life to help you carry the load.

Look up the following verses and discover some of the advantages of having Christian friends, especially when life is getting the best of you.

Romans 12:15

What does this say about your relationships with your brothers and sisters in Christ?

Romans 15:1

Put this verse in your own words.

Galatians 6:1-2

What would these verses look like in real life if we obeyed this command? Give an example of how carrying a burden might work out in someone's life.

Have you ever experienced the truths of these verses in your life? Take a minute and list the top three people in your life with whom you feel safe in sharing your hurts and struggles:

1.

2.

3.

What qualities do these people have that make them so special to you? Give these people a call whenever you're hurting—that's what they're there for!

When I am hurting and confused about life, I should share my struggles with a Christian friend.

First Things First

Fly with the Angels

Without debate, the greatest professional football team of the sixties was the Green Bay Packers. Perhaps the number one reason the Packers were such winners can be traced back to their coach, Vince Lombardi. Emulated by today's NFL coaches, Lombardi had the uncanny ability to bring out the best in his men. Through his leadership, they became more than just players running a play. They were men following their leader. But sometimes following that leader came at inconvenient times.

Once, after a disappointing loss on the road, Coach Lombardi was thinking of a way to teach his team a valuable lesson about their unexpected loss. Believing they had not given their best, the coach had the team taken by bus back to their home turf, Lambeau Field. In the dead of a cruel Wisconsin winter, with the temperature well below freezing, he unloaded his team out onto the freezing turf. Gathering them around him, he began, "Gentlemen, this is a football. . . ." And with those words, practice began.

Like those players, we experience defeat in our lives because we lose sight of the basics. Our priorities get out of order. And when this happens, sometimes depression and sadness can result. When we don't seek God's kingdom first, we will be miserable and sad (Psalm 16:4; Matthew 6:33). To help us get back to the basics, let's go to the practice field.

Paul gave his disciple Timothy some wise advice. Let's peek at his second letter to Timothy and see what it was.

Dear Tim,

Hey, bud! What's up? I know you've been discouraged lately, so I thought I would drop you a note to encourage you. Here are some ways you can keep your spiritual life and your priorities in order.

1. Fight like a _____
   (2 Timothy 2:3–4)
2. Compete like an _____
   (2 Timothy 2:5)
3. Work like a_____
   (2 Timothy 2:3–6)

Do this, and I promise God will bless you. Take care, and I hope to see you soon.

Your friend,

Paul

Why do you think it would be foolish for a soldier to entangle himself in the affairs of everyday life? Key Word—FOCUS.

How does a winning athlete compete, according to verse 5? Key Word—OBEDIENCE.

How is the farmer described in verse 6? And what does he receive when he does this? Key Word—REWARD.

Remember:
1. FOCUS
2. OBEDIENCE
3. REWARD

In other words, when we make the things that are important to God important to us, he will honor that. So when you're going through trials, it's essential to keep studying your Bible, praying, going to church, witnessing, praising God, and encouraging others—all the things you'd be doing if things were going great. Just keep doing the basics, not because you feel like it (you probably won't), but because that's where your strength will come from.

Is there any priority in your life that needs to be rearranged today? Is there any sin that needs to be confessed to help you do that?

Could there be
- an unspiritual relationship?
- an unhealthy friendship?
- a sinful habit?
- a bad attitude?
- apathy?
- pride?
- impure thoughts?
- sexual sin?

Where is God on your priority list right now? If someone watched your life for a week or two, what would they say are the things you think are most important?

Ordering your priorities and putting God in his rightful place gives you joy in the middle of hard times (see Isaiah 26:3; John 14:27; 16:33). Take a minute and identify your top five priorities. Choose from the following list or come up with your own: Jesus, School, Work, Family, Friends, Boyfriend or Girlfriend, College, Sports, Car, Grades, Cheerleading, Church, Music, Possessions, etc.

Write your list on a self-stick note and place it on your bathroom mirror or inside your locker. It will remind you to keep first things first.

TAKE-AWAY THOUGHT

When I keep my priorities in order, I will experience joy and God's blessing in my life.

Whatever It Takes

Fly with the Angels

Harry Truman (no relation to the president by that name) lived near the foot of Mount Saint Helens in 1980. In spite of the official warnings that the volcano could erupt at any time, Harry was determined that no one would persuade him to evacuate his home. Mr. Truman remained on his front porch, rocking back and forth in his favorite chair. Even when the gigantic volcano began to rumble, he stayed put, ignoring the facts and never believing anything would happen. But old Harry should have used common sense. On May 18, 1980, Mount Saint Helens erupted with a force equivalent to ten million tons of TNT, or about five hundred atomic bombs! The sound from this explosion was so loud that it was heard in other countries. Whatever happened to Harry? As far as we know, he still could be sitting on his front porch, buried under tons of mud and ash.

Harry Truman had determination. He had persistence, steadfastness, and bulldoglike characteristics. Great qualities to have when channeled in the right direction. Harry, however, was stubborn to a fault. God doesn't want you to be like Harry. Rather, he wants you to be determined about the right things—namely, not giving up on your spiritual life. He wants you to never give up, to be persistent, steadfast, and bulldoglike in your faith.

Is there something you've done that took determination and persistence? What was it?

Think back to that accomplishment. What made you so determined? What kept you plugging away?

Are you glad you didn't give up?

Unfortunately, giving up was exactly what young Timothy was about to do. He was discouraged about his life and ministry. He felt defeated. In fact, there is evidence that he was about to quit serving God altogether. So his spiritual big brother Paul wrote to encourage him and to persuade Timothy to hang in there.

Read 2 Timothy 2:8-10. Why do you think Paul's personal experience would encourage Timothy?

What do you think it means to endure something?

In what ways does Paul's advice in 2 Timothy 4:5 apply to you?

By enduring hardships in God's strength, what was Paul able to say? Why do you think he could say this? (2 Timothy 4:7)

Rewrite 2 Timothy 4:7 in your own words.

When you hang in there, especially during the tough times, you're not denying the problems and struggles. It means that you aren't weighed down by your difficulties. Instead of being slowed down spiritually, you have the supernatural ability to rise above your problems.

In the nineteenth century, a young boy desperately wanted to be a writer. He wasn't too confident because he didn't have a formal education or a good family life. So he went to work putting labels on bottles in an old warehouse. With enough money to sleep in an attic with other poor boys, this young man spent his spare time writing. Day after day he wrote, until finally he got up enough courage to submit a manuscript to a publisher. Weeks later, the publisher wrote back, rejecting his manuscript. Time and time again he submitted his writings, and each time the answer was the same—rejection. But this young boy refused to quit. He was determined that nothing would stop him.

Finally, one of his stories was accepted. He didn't receive any money for the story, but he walked down the streets of his town overjoyed that his story would be published. Because of his "whatever it takes" attitude, in just a few years all of England was reading his stories. That young boy who refused to quit was Charles Dickens, one of the greatest novelists who ever lived.

Which of these statements best describes you?

- I give up easily.
- I quit when things don't go my way.
- I tend to get discouraged a lot.
- I hang in there during most circumstances.
- I need to be more spiritually "tough."
- I can endure a lot and still be content.
- I am a spiritually consistent and faithful person.
- I hardly ever give up.

Think about your spiritual life.

What slows you down spiritually?

What keeps you from living 100 percent for Christ?

What puts the brakes on your desire for God?

What knocks you off track?

What douses your fire for God?

What does it take to make you want to give up?

Whatever it is, you have to let it go. You must determine that nothing will stop you from following Jesus. If you really want to finish the race as Paul did, you must choose to have a never-say-die attitude.

TAKE-AWAY THOUGHT

I must never give up following Christ, no matter what happens.

CHAPTER FIVE

Take Me to the Cross

She's Daddy's little girl
Only three years old
All dressed up in her Sunday clothes
He held her hand on bended knee
He said I need to show you how
To find your way home

As they walked along, how sweet the sound
Church bells ringing, people gathered 'round
He said remember this church
And the cross way up there
Sweetheart, if you ever get lost say:

Chorus:
Take me to the cross
High upon the steeple
The one where Jesus died
For all the lost people (For all the hurting people)
If you can't find home
Know you're not alone
Take me to the cross

As the years went by
Daddy's little girl
Lost herself in a big, big world
Then on the day her daddy died
She said I need to know why

[repeat chorus]

Now that same little girl
Thirty years gone by
She still knows Daddy's by her side
She raises her boy
In her father's way
And smiles when she hears him say

[repeat chorus]

Bridge over Troubled Water

Take Me to the Cross

The Royal Gorge Bridge in Colorado is the highest bridge in the world. It towers 1,053 feet above the Arkansas River and spans some 880 feet across. No wonder people freak out when they try to cross this bridge. If you're afraid of heights, then you might as well forget this tourist spot on your next vacation.

But there is another bridge you need to check out. It's not a man-made structure, but a spiritual bridge. Many people start the walk across the bridge but never make it. Doubts, fears, and hard times keep a lot of Christian teenagers from making it all the way across this bridge. But if you do make it across the bridge, then you probably have a firm grasp of who Jesus is and what he wants you to do. It means you stand for all that is involved in Christianity. You won't cross this bridge in a day. It takes time. It takes dedication and faith. There is no room to stand still on this bridge. You must decide whether or not you will move forward or turn back.

Which way are you heading today?

Today's devotion will help you understand if the faith you profess is really yours yet.

Every Christian has someone who has helped him or her understand more about the Christian life. Who has helped you in your walk of faith?

- My parents
- My friends (which ones?)
- My youth pastor
- My pastor
- Sunday school teachers, group leaders, and others
- Other miscellaneous people

Find and read 2 Timothy 1:5.

From whom did Timothy learn about faith in God?

When did this all begin for Timothy? (3:14-15)

What kinds of attitudes do you think you need in order to learn from someone else?

What would you say it means to be convinced of something?

Who else had a huge part in Timothy's spiritual growth? What did he do for young Timothy? (1:13; 2:1-2)

Take me as an example. There was a time in my life when I thought I was a Christian, but I wasn't sure. I was very religious at church and around my Christian friends. I was a leader in my youth group, and I felt it was my responsibility to set a good example for others. But sometimes at school and on the weekends, I didn't feel like much of a Christian. My approach to God was like getting dressed in the morning—I wore what I thought would make me look good and feel good that day. In other words, I dressed for the part. Have you ever felt as I did?

If the truth were known, many teenagers who attend church are simply borrowing someone else's faith—it could be their parents' faith or their friends' faith— perhaps because Christianity meets a social or emotional need in their lives at the time. It's like borrowing money or clothes or a CD from a friend, only to give it back when you're done with it or when it no longer serves its purpose.

You may be thinking, *So how can I know if what I say I believe is really what I believe? How can I know the difference between "renting" my faith and actually owning it?*

It's like the difference between the way people treat things they rent—like cars, golf clubs, skates, skis—and the way they treat things they own. Many times, if something belongs to someone else, people might abuse it, take it for granted, or mistreat it. But if it belongs to them, they treat it with great care and responsibility.

The following is a checklist—a sort of personal inventory—to see how much of your faith is really yours. Check the descriptions that fit you and your spiritual life.

RENTERS	*versus*	OWNERS
• Ho-hum, apathetic about spiritual things		• Eager to grow and learn. Want to know more.
• Enjoy doing Bible studies only if they don't get too deep		• Desire depth
• Motivated from the outside; need a jump start and have to be enticed with fun activities at church		• Motivated from the heart; don't have to be begged to participate in spiritual things
• Inconsistent, sporadic, casual commitment		• Faithful, consistent, can be counted on
• Have a two-faced faith—one kind of person at church, and totally different at school and on weekends		• Are genuine and real—no matter where and who they're with
• Only interested in the benefits of Christianity; ask, "What's in it for me?"		• Are interested in serving others; ask, "How can I help?"
• Don't last—chuck faith, usually losing interest during high school or college		• Keep going—cross over to the other side of the bridge

Do you see the difference between renting and owning your faith? What about you? Where are you on this spiritual bridge we've been talking about? Are you closer to the renting end or the owning end?

Are you currently

- moving forward spiritually?
- going backwards?
- standing still?

Stop for a moment and pray about those areas where you're still renting your faith. Talk to God about those areas and give them to him. Ask him for his strength to deal with them. Ask, "Lord, what do I need to do in my life in order to move on toward maturity?"

Write out a plan of action:

- *Area*
- *Action*

- *Area*
- *Action*

- *Area*
- *Action*

TAKE-AWAY THOUGHT

When I am committed to spiritual growth, my faith becomes my own.

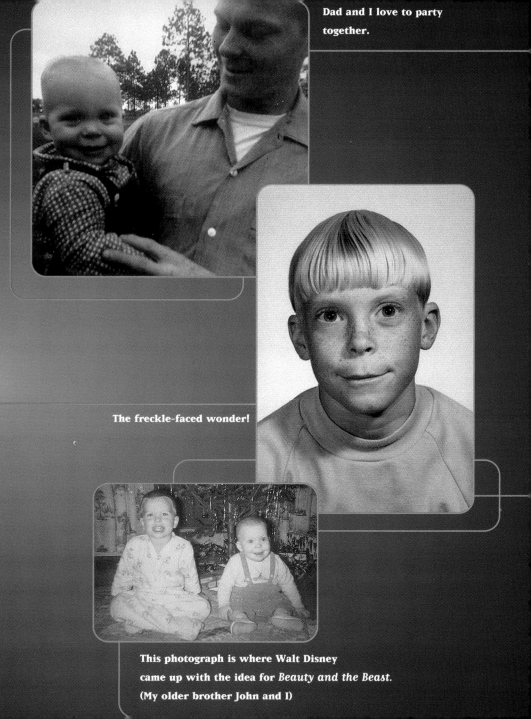

Dad and I love to party together.

The freckle-faced wonder!

This photograph is where Walt Disney came up with the idea for *Beauty and the Beast.* (My older brother John and I)

Mary Damron
and I help Amir
explore the contents
of his gift box.
Look at that smile!

I met Amir at an
army concert hall
in Sarajevo.
His father was killed
in the fighting.
His mother was
killed in a gas
explosion that left
him badly scarred.

I was honored to be a part
of the Operation Christmas Child
team that brought shoe-box gifts
to this primary school in Bosnia.

The Dream Team
(Dad had to take the picture.)

My first guitar . . .

Can you guess what's in this box?
(I forgot.)

After my first day of skiing in Tahoe, the only thing still in one piece was my smile.

My first public kiss in the ninth grade. I kissed both girls!

My parents bought a piano for me to practice on
(in college).

Opening a concert
for Wayne Watson
and Russ Taff
in Houston.
(January 1985)

A Great American Tradition

USO SHOWS
presents
Fantasy

Date
Time
Place

Fast
and
Funny
DISCO
Revue

Armed Forces Entertainment

Eighteen years old and my first
professional tour with Bob Hope USO Tours.

Living the Difference

Take Me to the Cross

William Cush, a passenger agent for the Missouri, Kansas, and Texas Railroad, proposed that the railroad stage a train crash as a publicity stunt. Calling it the "Monster Head-On Collision," Mr. Cush took two old steam locomotives, gave them a fresh coat of paint, and then hooked six cars to each.

On September 15, 1896, the day for the stunt arrived. A circus tent was erected, and by 10:00 A.M. ten thousand people had gathered; the crowd swelled to forty thousand by the afternoon. At 5:20 P.M., the trains came thundering down the track and collided in an awful crash. The boilers from both trains immediately exploded, sending debris and metal splinters in every direction. Two men were killed and many others were injured, including a photographer who lost an eye capturing the historic crash on film.

People haven't changed much. We still love to gawk at tragedy and disaster. We have this morbid curiosity about other people's tragedies, and their scandals in particular. Especially if the scandal involves a religious leader.

The world is quick to condemn a Christian who preaches one thing and lives another. The Bible calls it hypocrisy. The word *hypocrite* comes from the ancient Greek plays, where a person would wear a mask in a play, pretending to be someone he was not. There are hypocrites everywhere—at school, on the team, in the classroom, at work, and in the neighborhood—but nowhere do hypocrites stand out more than they do in church.

Today's study is all about helping you avoid hypocrisy. It will show you the different lifestyle Christ wants his followers to have, and how as a Christian you can live out that difference in your life.

Read Ephesians 2:1-5.

Some people have dramatic testimonies of how they became Christians, and some of us who came to know Christ at an early age, well, our testimonies are boring, right? Not exactly. The Bible says that Christ did the exact same thing in you as he did in every other believer's life. The bottom line is that no matter what your conversion experience, you are not the same person you used to be when you are in Christ.

From the verses you just read, jot down as many things as you can that describe your old life before you became a Christian.

- _____
- _____
- _____
- _____
- _____
- _____

Now turn a few pages over to Ephesians 4:17-19. Describe the lifestyle of people who do not know God.

Describe the lifestyle of people who do know God (see Ephesians 4:20-24).

It's like this: God wants the world to see a difference between those who are his children and those who are not. Dogs and cats act differently. Horses, cows, fish, and birds all act differently from each other. Why? Because of their nature, or how they're made. Animals are just acting naturally.

A farmer had a pet pig that he loved very much. The pig had won many blue ribbons in livestock shows, and the farmer was very proud of him. Because he was so fond of the pig, the farmer decided to let his prized porker live inside the house. But his wife (the smart one in the family) objected to this idea, complaining about the awful smell and foul habits of pigs. To convince his wife otherwise, the farmer took his pig down to the local beauty shop and had him bathed, groomed, and manicured. He even had a little shirt made for his pig. The final touch was a splash of cologne. The farmer brought the pig home, proudly presenting him to his wife. At first his wife was hesitant, but finally she gave in and let the pig move in.

Later that afternoon, while watching TV with the farmer, the pig suddenly jumped up and ran out the back door and straight to a fresh mud puddle, where he wallowed for a long time before falling asleep. The farmer was shocked. He didn't understand. He thought his pet was special. He was angry at the pig. But his wife simply came over to him, put her arm around his shoulder, and said, "Dear, you just have to realize that a pig is a pig. It can't be anything but a pig, and you can't change that. He's just doing what is natural. Pigs like dirt, mud, and slop, not perfume, clothes, and being indoors."

Even though we're not pigs, before we became Christians we were controlled by our old sin nature. We could never change who we really were inside or be anything different on our own no matter how much we changed the outside. When God saved us, he changed our nature. He changed us from the inside out. That's also why the Bible says we are "new persons" (2 Corinthians 5:17). We are different.

Exactly what does it mean to have a changed nature? Look at Ephesians again and find out how God says that should affect your

- *speech (4:25, 29; 5:4)?*
- *emotions (4:26-27)?*
- *relationships (4:31-32)?*
- *purity (5:1-3)?*

Remember, even though you were once in darkness, God now says you are a child of light and should live like one (Ephesians 5:8-9).

I am not
the person
I used to be.
God has made
me into a
new person!

Impact!

Take Me to the Cross

Some thousands of years ago, something came rocketing through our atmosphere and crashed into the earth. The crater, near Canyon Diablo, Winslow, Arizona, is known as the Barrington Crater and was discovered in 1891. This crater is an impressive 575 feet deep and 4,150 feet in diameter. The sides, or rims, of the massive crater rise 150 feet above the surrounding plain. For years, scientists have debated about what kind of object could have made the crater because there is hardly any trace of outer-space debris in the crater. Some experts today have speculated that an asteroid no wider than a few yards crashed into the canyon plain at such a high speed that it not only caused the giant crater but also disintegrated in the process!

I know what you're thinking. How could something so small leave such a large crater? How could it possibly have left that great of a dent in the earth?

Answer: Impact.

A general rule of physics is that the greater the impact, the greater the mark left behind. But it's not just true in physics and asteroids. The same laws apply to your relationships as well. You can make an impact on your campus and leave your mark for God through your friendships. Most of what you experience in life happens in the context of relationships. Without friends (especially our Christian friends), life would be extremely dull. True friends are a gift from God. They are the ones who help you walk with the Lord. You love them, and they love you. And how do you spell love? T-I-M-E. Friends plus time equals impact. Your buddies and you can help each other in your mutual faith, and you can influence other people for Christ too.

In the Old Testament, there was a man who was a true friend. His name was Elijah. He was a prophet and spoke for God to the people. Even though Elijah spent a lot of time by himself, he still made the time to be a friend to some "prophets in training." One of those would-be prophets was a young man named Elisha. As you look at the final days of their friendship together, you can learn a lot about what it means to have a godly influence on others.

Find 2 Kings, chapter 2, and read verses 1-6. What is the first thing you notice about the relationship of Elijah and Elisha?

Think about it. Your friends wouldn't be your friends if you didn't spend time together. These two guys really enjoyed being with each other. There was a bond between them. In fact, Elisha wanted to go with Elijah wherever he went (vv. 2, 4, 6).

What are some things you have in common with your closest friends?

A fierce storm hit a small southern town. Winds were gusting at near-hurricane velocity. When the wind and the rain had passed, almost all the trees in the town had been blown over—except for a group of trees in the town park. Most of the leaves had blown off the trees and several branches had broken off, but these trees stood strong and tall. These trees' roots had spread out under the surface and interlocked with each other. Because of this subterranean strength, literally nothing was able to blow the trees over. By locking roots, they made each other stronger.

Your Christian friendships can be like those trees. And the friendship between Elijah and Elisha was like that. It went far beyond shallow talk and just hanging out. Like those trees, their roots were deeply intertwined below the surface. And that made the two prophets strong, stable, and secure. But what else made them strong?

Look at 2 Kings 2:7-8.

What did Elisha see Elijah do in these verses?

Elijah knew he was in a situation where God was going to test and strengthen their faith. Because he had the power, Elijah performed this miracle. Elijah and Elisha (not to mention the other prophet interns) witnessed the power of God together. Together they saw God do things only he could do.

In what ways have your Christian friends motivated you to grow in your relationship with Christ?

In what ways have you "experienced God" together?

How can your Christian friendships help you make a lasting impact for God on your campus?

Leave your mark, and make it a huge one!

Together, my Christian friends and I can have a huge influence for God on our campus.

Passing the Torch
Take Me to the Cross

Have you ever noticed how many kids wear authentic game jerseys? If it's a team sport, college or professional, somebody's wearing the jersey. People like to identify with a winning team or the star player. How many times have you imitated Michael Jordan as you go up for a basket? It's common for people to imitate their heroes. They want to be like people who have excelled in their fields and to follow their examples. It's normal to look up to your heroes.

Elijah was like a hero to Elisha. Elisha had learned a lot about life from Elijah. He saw real faith and devotion to God modeled right before his eyes, and he wanted that for himself. He saw what it meant to be used by God in a mighty way, and he wanted that. He saw how people were drawn to the Lord as a result of being around Elijah, and he wanted that. He wanted what Elijah had. He wanted to live the kind of life Elijah lived. He wanted to be like Elijah.

As Elijah ministered, Elisha watched him like a hawk. He was taking notes on Elijah's life, and the prophet knew it. Elijah probably considered himself to be a spiritual "big brother" to Elisha.

What about you?

Who are you watching? Whose life are you looking at and taking notes on? Who do you want to be like?

That's great. But have you ever wondered if someone is watching you? In reality, there is a good chance that several people are looking to you as their spiritual example. They see you at church, at school, at your locker, at the mall, on the field, on the court, at work, at home, and out on the weekends. They may be your closest friends or only acquaintances, or you may not know them at all. They may be in your class, or they may be a grade or two below you. But they're watching. Not because they're trying to see if you mess up, but because they respect you. They see something in you they want to imitate. In a sense, they see in you what Elisha saw in Elijah.

They see God.

Now let's wrap up our story. Finally, it came time for Elijah to leave the earth and leave behind his young disciple Elisha. But before he left, Elijah asked if there was anything more he could do for Elisha.

What did Elisha request? (2 Kings 2:9)

What do you think Elisha was trying to say by this request? Was he power hungry? Did he want all the attention to be on him now that Elijah was leaving? Was he asking to be the man in charge of all the prophets? What do you suppose he was really trying to say?

Elijah said that the power God had given him could be passed on to Elisha. But there was a condition. What was it? (v. 10)

Then Elijah went to heaven in a chariot of fire (vv. 10-11). Talk about your dramatic exits! Elisha saw the exit and went on to do many great miracles through God. His life was marked by great power and was a demonstration of God's glory. Even after he died, Elisha still had power. A dead man was accidentally cast into the grave of Elisha, and when the dead man touched Elisha's bones, he came back to life (see 2 Kings 13:20-21)!

What had the prophet Elijah given to Elisha? He gave him a life worth imitating. He was able to say, like the apostle Paul, "Follow my example" (1 Corinthians 4:16; 11:1; see also 2 Thessalonians 3:9).

Who is your Elijah or Paul? (Who are you watching?)

Who is your Elisha or Timothy? (Who is watching you?)

Think ahead to the day when you will graduate. You're standing in line, waiting to receive your diploma. Your palms are sweating (you hope no one knows about that overdue library book). Your parents, relatives, and friends are all there. You're thinking about how you've worked hard for years, and in a few minutes you'll actually graduate. Afterward there'll be parties and pictures, but also good-byes.

Have you ever thought about your mark on your school years? Will your legacy be a yearbook photo? A senior will? Some fond memories? Your name carved in a tree somewhere on campus or written in a textbook? What about your senior class? What will they remember you for? What about those still in school?

Wouldn't it be great to leave behind a legacy of faith? Wouldn't it be great to pass the torch of Christianity on to those who will keep it burning at your school?

The good news is that you can do that, and it's a lot easier than you think. How will you pass on the torch of Christianity, beginning this week?

Write down some personal goals to shoot for this year to help you pass the torch.

- _____
- _____
- _____
- _____
- _____

Perhaps God is telling you to take someone "to the cross." Write that person's name down here, and begin to think of how you will tell about Christ.

_____

Pass the gospel torch on, and you will be sure to pass it down to others. You can do it!

TAKE-AWAY THOUGHT

I can leave a legacy of faith to those behind me.

90

Look Who I Found!
Take Me to the Cross

When I was in high school, two friends and I took some groceries to an elderly man and his brother who lived in an old farmhouse in the country. We had heard they needed food, and we wanted to help them out. When we got there, we discovered that the two brothers, both in their eighties, were pretty poor, and the only source of heat in the house was from a pot-belly stove.

After giving them the groceries, we sat down to talk with the brothers. I was talking with one of the brothers, and my friends were talking to the other man. As we talked, the conversation turned to spiritual things. When I realized that the old man didn't have a relationship with God, I shared the gospel with him and explained what Christ had done for him. Unfortunately, he didn't want to ask Jesus to be his Savior. Sadly, about six months later, the old man died. Out of respect and kindness, my friends and I attended the funeral. We saw the old man's brother there. As he reflected on his brother's death and the shortness of his own life, this brother humbly opened his heart to the Lord and became a Christian. We were very happy for him, but also a bit sad that it took his brother's death to make him realize his need for God. In a strange way, his brother had brought him to Jesus.

Today you're going to look at another pair of brothers, and how one brother brought the other to Jesus.

Read John 1:35-37. These verses talk about two disciples of John the Baptist. We don't know both their names, but one of them was Andrew, Simon Peter's brother (v. 40).

When John the Baptist pointed Jesus out to his followers, what did Andrew immediately do? (v. 37)

What was the next step in his relationship with Jesus? (vv. 38-39)

Why do you think Andrew wanted to do this?

In Bible times a disciple was a learner and a follower. Disciples in those days would literally sit at their teacher's feet to learn from him. They would follow him wherever he went, watching his life, learning from him, imitating his actions, and reproducing his teachings in the lives of others.

Like a good disciple, what did Andrew do next? (vv. 41-42)

What happened to Simon Peter as a result of this? (v. 42)

Andrew had never taken a course in witnessing. He didn't even have a gospel tract or a Bible. He simply told his brother that he had found the Messiah, and then brought Simon Peter to him.

You can't exactly bring people to Jesus the way Andrew did, since Jesus isn't physically walking around with us. So what are some ways you can still bring people to Jesus today?

In 1900 in Beaumont, Texas, several wealthy investors came to town to drill for oil, which they were convinced was somewhere deep underground just south of town. So in October of that year, they hired the Hamill brothers—Al, Jim, and Curt—to start drilling for oil. First the brothers hit quicksand and then rock. But they kept on drilling, straight through until Christmas and into the new year.

Finally, on January 10, 1901, their drill got stuck at 1,020 feet below the surface. As they were replacing the drill bit, mud began boiling up out of the hole. Then, *kaboom!* Mud and rock shot up out of the ground and into the air, followed by a massive geyser of oil. The brothers were soaked. People came from miles around to see the spectacle. Soon the well was gushing eighty thousand barrels of oil a day. There was now only one problem—how to stop the flow. No one knew how to cap this monster. After nine days of brainstorming and nine million gallons of oil spewing out of the ground, the Hamill brothers risked their lives and capped the mighty oil well, now known in history as Spindletop.

Many times when someone becomes a Christian, he or she is like that oil well—overflowing with praise for what God has done for him or her. In fact, the person can't stop talking about Jesus. Then it happens. The person calms down, his or her mouth is capped, and the person becomes quiet about the Lord.

Don't you think it's time to take the cap off and start gushing a little more about him?

So who do you need to tell about Jesus?

- *Family member*
- *Friend*
- *Classmate*
- *Teammate*
- *Coworker*
- *Relative*

Write down their names, and spend some time today praying about how you are going to bring them to Jesus.

Remember, people *take people to the Cross.*

TAKE-AWAY THOUGHT

I should never stop bringing others to Jesus.

CHAPTER SIX

The Road Less Travelled

To follow what you've never seen isn't easy
Guess it all comes down to a matter of faith
My destination is where Jesus leads me
Wherever he's goin', I'm gonna walk that way

Channel:
Not gonna follow the masses down the path that's wide
Don't wanna bear my regret on the other side

Chorus:
*The road less travelled is not easy street
But it leads to a place where faith and glory meet
It carries the sinner to the mercy seat
I wanna feel the road less travelled beneath my feet*

Sometimes I go for miles without a sign
Wondering how far it is I've got to go
With nothing but a promise, I take it in stride
'Cause you gotta believe to walk this road

Bridge:
I want a heart of hope
Feet of faith
The will to keep walkin'
Come what may . . .

[repeat chorus]

The Demands of Discipleship DAY 22
The Road Less Travelled

The great Blondin (real name Jean-François Gravelet) had the greatest high-wire act in the world. In the 1800s, thousands of people were thrilled by his death-defying walks across the tightrope. Perhaps his most dramatic and daring walks were the ones across Niagara Falls. Before as many as ten thousand spectators, the fair-haired aerialist would balance himself on a two-inch-thick rope stretched from one side to the other of the eleven-hundred-foot walk.

Blondin would cross the Niagara on a bicycle, on stilts, and even do his stunts at night. He would turn somersaults and stand on his head, while balanced on a chair. One time he even pushed a wheelbarrow across and cooked an omelet. Blondin would turn to the crowd and offer to carry anyone across. Very few people ever took him up on his offer. But on occasion a daring soul would step forward. Gripping a thirty-five-foot balancing pole, Blondin would carry the volunteer across the rope.

Blondin's bravery is legendary, but what about the people who trusted the great French aerialist to carry them across the rope? Imagine how they must have had to rely completely on Blondin's ability to carry them safely across. They knew the danger, but they had complete confidence in the great Blondin. They were totally committed to him.

There is a passage in Luke's Gospel where Jesus asks his followers to make a similar commitment to him. His demands might even be considered more risky than crossing Niagara Falls on a man's back. See what you think.

Turn to Luke 14:25-27.

What does Jesus ask you to do in verse 26? (For a further explanation, see Matthew 10:37.)

What do you think he meant by that statement?

What else does he say you are to hate?

What other requirement for discipleship does he give? (v. 27)

A cross in those days meant death.

Why do you suppose Jesus talked this way to such a large crowd? Do you think it made anyone think twice about following Jesus? Why?

On December 7, 1941, a Japanese plane crash-landed on the deck of an American ship docked at Pearl Harbor, Hawaii. Surprisingly, the plane did not explode on impact. An American sailor rushed to yank the cockpit door off the downed plane, and to his amazement he saw a petrified fifteen-year-old Japanese boy! The American sailor then noticed the young pilot was a kamikaze. This young man had been ordered to fly his plane headfirst into that ship. Taking off that Sunday morning, the young pilot had left on a

one-way mission he knew would end in death on the deck of an American ship. That's how committed he was to the Japanese emperor's cause. He wasn't trying out the Japanese military to see if he liked it. He was sold out. He was dedicated. He was devoted. He knew there was no turning back.

It all boils down to one word—*commitment*. Jesus wants you to be totally committed to him and him alone. Unless he has all of your heart, you won't follow him for very long. No one can serve two masters. Your heart has only one throne. There is room for only one person to sit on that throne and call the shots in your life.

Who do you love more than anyone?

- Mom
- Dad
- A brother or sister
- A girlfriend or boyfriend
- Yourself

Who is really in control of your life? Who's sitting on the throne?

How much of you does Jesus actually have rule over?
- *25%*
- *50%*
- *75%*
- *100%*

If you are a Christian, you must be totally, 100-percent committed to Christ and to him alone. There must be no greater love in your life. In fact, you must love him more than you love life itself. Sound demanding? That's because it is. Sound scary? Not really. But you must trust him enough to step off the safety of the firm ground and onto the rope. Climb on his back and place complete confidence in his ability, and he will carry you safely to the other side.

Jesus demands all of me if I want to call myself his disciple.

Counting the Cost

The Road Less Travelled

Once I took my wife to a very expensive French restaurant for Valentine's Day. Thinking of myself as quite the romantic, I figured we would enjoy a candlelit dinner and a special evening. I thought I was a real big spender. You see, I had a whopping fifty dollars. After being seated, my first clue that I was in trouble was when the waiter (with the funny accent) handed the menu to me. It had no prices on it. But no problem, I had fifty bucks. We ordered an appetizer, then came the main course, and it was great. After that was dessert. Three hours later, our waiter brought me the bill. At first I was afraid to look, but how bad could it be?

Well, unlike my menu, the bill did have a price on it—to the tune of $110. My heart began to race. I broke out into a cold sweat. All I had was fifty dollars, my checkbook, and a gas credit card (and I was sure they didn't carry unleaded gasoline!). I quietly wrote a slightly warm check and made a mad dash for the door. Now I was a broke romantic. I learned an important lesson that night: Always count the cost before ordering.

As Jesus traveled the countryside in his day, he urged those who followed him to take a long look at the menu he offered them. Jesus was very up-front with people about what it would cost to follow him. He wants each of us to make sure we understand the price of being his disciple.

In Luke 14:28-35, Jesus helps us understand that cost with three illustrations of what it means to follow him. What are those illustrations?

Illustration 1 (vv. 28-30)

Illustration 2 (vv. 31-32)

Illustration 3 (vv. 34-35)

Now try to finish these three short sayings to fit the illustrations.

Don't start what you can't _____ or you'll be a laughingstock.

It is best to make _____ with a superior king, or you will certainly be conquered by him.

If you're salt, then you ought to be _____ otherwise you're useless.

A small house-church in an eastern European country met in secret because the government didn't allow the worship of God. One afternoon as the tiny group of believers was meeting quietly, the door burst open and two government soldiers crashed the meeting. Waving machine guns, they commanded all the church members to line up against the wall to be executed. Just before they squeezed the triggers, the soldiers said, "Anyone who wants to deny his or her faith in God will be allowed to leave unharmed."

After a short pause, a handful of people scurried out of the house. Then the guards closed the doors behind them, laid down their guns, and explained, "We, too, are followers of Jesus. But we wanted to know who else was a true believer in him. You see, we believe that you are not ready to live for our Lord until you are ready to die for him."

The church members who left didn't count the cost of what it meant to follow Christ in their country. They were like the builder who wasn't able to finish. What Jesus was trying to do in this passage was to weed out people who weren't really serious about a relationship with him. Think about it. If following Christ was easy, everybody would be doing it! If it didn't cost anything, everybody would want it!

Have you thought through what kind of cost and commitment it's going to take to follow Christ for the rest of your life?

What do you think following Christ would cost you in your
- family?
- school?
- circle of friends?
- country?

TAKE-AWAY THOUGHT

It's a serious thing to follow Christ, so I must count the cost.

Building on the Rock

The Road Less Travelled

*D*uring the construction of the Quebec Bridge in 1907, something horribly unexpected happened. Late in the afternoon on August 29, a steelworker perched high on the bridge above the water heard a loud noise that sounded like the blast of a cannon. At that very moment, the largest section of the massive structure suddenly collapsed, sending nineteen thousand tons of steel crashing into the Saint Lawrence River. Of the eighty-six men who were working on the bridge at the time, seventy-five were killed instantly.

Later, after an extensive investigation, it was learned that the fateful bridge was destined to collapse from the start. Investigators found serious flaws in the original design. As a result, it was built improperly and caused a terrible tragedy.

As awful as something like that is, even worse is the way some people's lives collapse under the stress and strain of everyday life. Lives are destroyed because people are basing their values and priorities on faulty designs. There are fatal flaws in their thinking and lifestyles that lead to devastating consequences. Jesus knew all about faulty foundations, and in Matthew 7:24-27 he told a short story about two kinds of people. See what comparisons and contrasts you can find between the two builders.

	Builder A		Builder B
_____	Heard Christ's words?		_____
_____	Put them into practice?		_____
_____	Rain, storm, and winds came?		_____
_____	House stood or fell?		_____
_____	Jesus described this builder as a		_____

What made the difference between the two builders?

What do you think the house in this story might represent?

According to Jesus, what will you be protected from if you build your life on his words?

What do you think your peers are building their lives on? Make a Top Ten list from these categories. Like David Letterman's list, start with number ten.

THE TOP TEN

Money	10.
Music	9.
Guy/girl relationships	8.
Sports	7.
Popularity	6.
Clothes	5.
Cars	4.
Sex	3.
Friendships	2.
Appearance	1.

Which of these ten would you say has too much importance in your life?

Think about it.
- Money can disappear in a moment.
- Music that's popular today may not be tomorrow.
- Guys and girls come and go.
- Sports last only for one season.
- Popularity fades.
- Clothes wear out.
- Cars break down.
- Sex outside of marriage doesn't satisfy.
- Friends will let you down.
- Outward appearance will change.

But the words of Christ last forever. They truly satisfy, and they never change. Build your life on his truths, and your house will stand through the storms.

What are some practical ways you can build your house on the words of Christ?

TAKE-AWAY THOUGHT

If I hear and obey Christ's words, I can face any storm life dumps on me.

The Real Thing

DAY 25

The Road Less Travelled

Have you ever heard of Norma Jean Baker or Madonna Louise Ciccone? Probably not, at least not by those names. When they entered show business, they changed their names as part of their image. You know them better as Marilyn Monroe and just Madonna.

It's not that big a deal to change your name for the public, but changing your actions to suit the crowd is.

> Back in the eighties, there was a man who was the master of disguises. He had the ability to portray himself as anyone he wanted to be. He even fooled the most intelligent people at the highest levels of their profession. Some of the disguises he put on were a surgeon (and actually performed an operation), a lawyer, and a commercial airline pilot.
>
> Law-enforcement officials to this day are still amazed that he not only was able to do something like this but also that he got away with it for so long.
>
> This man was a fake. A phony. A pretender. A cheap imitation of the real thing. He was what cubic zirconia is to diamonds. Like fake pearls or a phony Rolex. He may have looked the part on the outside, but when closely examined, he was an impostor.

Just like some Christians.

I was on a flight a while back, and my seatmate was a well-dressed business-man. We struck up a conversation, and I told him that I sang Christian music. "Are you a Christian?" I asked. The man immediately shot back, "No." When I asked him why he wasn't, he simply said, "Because I know too many Christians."

Ouch!

That man had a problem with people who don't practice what they preach. So did Jesus. In Matthew 7:13-14, Jesus divides life into two very separate categories. What are they?

| _____ Gate | _____ Gate |
| _____ Road | _____ Road |

Why do you think only a few people pass through the narrow gate and walk on the narrow road?

According to Jesus, how can you tell the difference between the two roads people are traveling on? (vv. 15-20)

What will happen to people who think they know the Lord but are really impostors? (vv. 21-23)

One of the twelve disciples, Judas Iscariot, is a prime example of someone who looked the part and played it well. Had he been an actor, he would have won an Academy Award. But he wasn't playing in a movie. He was one of the Master's chosen men. Posing as a dedicated disciple, he fooled them all, except Jesus. In the end, Judas's mask was lifted and his true colors were revealed. He was known by his fruit.

Not to be judgmental, but there are a lot of people today who say they're walking the narrow road when in reality they've never left the broad path. Like Judas, they go to church. Like him, they hear Jesus' teaching each week. Like him, they hang around other Christians. Everything is Christian on the outside, but deep down, in the places of their heart no one else sees, they really don't love God or want to follow him. They're impostors. Fakes. Like counterfeit money, they are not genuine. They're not real Christians.

How can you avoid that kind of hypocrisy in your own life? How can you keep from being a fake?

Simple. Jesus' wants to know you, to be your best friend, to have fellowship with you. Truly knowing Christ and staying close to him keeps you real and genuine, and prevents hypocrisy from dominating your life.

What are some ways you can grow in your relationship with Christ on a daily basis?

-
-
-

If you're doing those things right now, keep it up. And good going.

TAKE-AWAY THOUGHT

The more I seek to know Jesus in a personal way each day, the more I avoid spiritual phoniness.

There are certain things in life you should probably never do, such as

- answer your mother when she says, "What do you think I am? Stupid?"
- get change for a ten from money in the offering plate.
- blow a whole month's paycheck on that one stereo speaker.
- ask the girl you've been dating for two weeks to marry you.
- join the Marines in the tenth grade.
- run against your best friend for student-body president.
- tackle the book of Revelation the very first time you have devotions.
- skip school with the town's biggest loudmouth.
- eat something that's larger than your head.
- spike your hair before meeting your date's parents for the first time.

On the other hand, there are some things in life that you should do without even thinking. These are the times when you should jump in with both feet. For example:

- You have the basketball with three seconds left in the game—shoot!
- You caught a pass and there's nothing between you and the end zone—run!
- You know you're at a school-record pace with fifty meters to go—sprint!
- You win a free trip to Hawaii for you and five of your friends—go!
- You get your favorite mountain bike for your birthday—ride!
- You get asked out by the best-looking, godliest guy or girl in your class—duh!

When it comes to living the Christian life, we sometimes do the things we ought to be more cautious about, and hesitate about the things we ought to just go ahead and do. One of those things is exercising our faith. The Bible is crystal clear that we are to live by faith (Romans 1:17), but many times we hesitate. We procrastinate in the area of faith and end up missing out on God's best for us.

To help us avoid this, let's discover what faith really is and how we can take advantage of it in our daily lives.

> Look up Hebrews 11:1. Based on this verse, write your own definition of what faith is.

> What example does the writer give in verse 3?

Faith is being sure of something you can't see. Like the creation of the world. Since we weren't there to see it happen, we have to exercise faith to believe that God merely spoke it into existence just like his Word says he did. It's a matter of trust, isn't it?

You and I exercise faith every day.

- We turn on the light switch with the faith that the lights will come on.
- We sit in a chair with the faith that it will support us.
- We drive over a bridge with the faith that it will support the traffic.
- We eat food in restaurants with the faith that we won't get food poisoning.
- We order through catalogs with the faith that the company will send what we requested.

Have you ever thought of the faith you exercise when you get sick? You go to a doctor believing that the medical degrees on his walls are real and not fake.

You have faith that his diagnosis of your sickness (which you can't pronounce) is accurate. After being given a prescription you can't read, you go to a pharmacist and trust that the chemical compound he puts in your pills is exactly what you need for your sickness. Then you go home and take the pill! Now that's faith.

Why do we suddenly become afraid to trust God? Why is it so hard for us to trust him? Jot down any ideas you have.

A man was walking along a narrow path near a steep cliff. Not paying attention to what he was doing, he lost his balance and stumbled over the edge of the cliff. As he was falling, he managed to grab on to a branch. Now hanging in space between earth and sky, he wondered what he was going to do. After a few seconds, the branch started to crack, and the man began frantically calling for help.

Man: Is anybody up there?
Voice: Yes, I'm here!
Man: Who's that?
Voice: The Lord.
Man: Lord, help me! I can't hold on and the branch is breaking!
Voice: Do you trust me?
Man: I trust you completely, Lord.
Voice: Do you have faith that I will save you?
Man: Yes! I do have faith!
Voice: Good. Then let go of the branch.
Man: What???
Voice: I said to let go of the branch.
Man: [after a long pause] Is there anybody else up there?

Write about a time when you trusted God and he saw you through. Describe how you felt as you realized that God is totally trustworthy.

In what one area of your life do you need faith today? Ask God to increase your faith in that area, and he will.

I shouldn't hesitate to have faith in God, because he can be trusted with every area of my life.

CHAPTER SEVEN

The Choice

Tommy led his class in high school
Seemed he had everything
We all could see him going somewhere
'Til he crashed his dream
His girlfriend's father called him late one night
The news he heard would change his life

Chorus:
What you gonna do
What's it gonna take
For you to see wrong from right
How you gonna know
Where you're gonna go
Runnin' from your life
There's another way
There's another life
First you gotta see His truth

Tommy's story's too familiar
'Cause we all make mistakes
It's like you're racing down a mountain
And you've got no brakes
Before you find yourself where this road ends
It's time to make the choice, my friend

[repeat chorus]

Bridge:
In a world full of choices
There's one who understands
In your time of confusion
Look to Jesus

[repeat chorus]

So Many Choices

The Choice

Choices. Life is full of them. It's like life is one big multiple-choice exam, where "D. All of the above" isn't always a good choice. For example, see if you've had to make any of these choices lately:

- Go to the mall or over to a friend's house?
- Stay home or go to a movie?
- "Would you like fries with that?"
- Paper or plastic?
- CD or cassette?
- Shorts or jeans?
- Boots or sneakers?
- Study or talk on the phone?
- Go to church or sleep in?

Or what about all the choices you make at school? Test your knowledge with this multiple-choice exam [on the next page].

OK, enough choices! The point is that life is a series of choices, one fork in the road after another. Today you will learn why the choices you make each day are important and how they can change your life. Hang on, here we go.

Here's the plot for a great miniseries. He was young, handsome, rich, and powerful. He had everything a man could want, including a great reputation. He was the stuff of which legends were made. He was the topic of folklore—a giant-killer, a brave heart, a courageous warrior, a fearless fighter, the hero of bedtime stories

1. Who invented the turtleneck sweater?

a) Attila the Hun
b) Attila the Nun
c) Alexander the Great
d) Frank the not-so-great
e) Caesar
f) Caesar salad
g) The turtle
h) Who knows?
i) Who cares?

2. Where in the Bible would you find 1 John 1:9?

a) In the book of 2 Condominiums
b) In the fifth chapter of Barnacles
c) Near 2 John 1:9
d) Somewhere near the maps
e) Could you repeat the question?

3. Who said, "The only thing we have to fear is fear itself"?

a) Franklin D. Roosevelt
b) Barney Fife
c) Indiana Jones
d) Your history teacher
e) Your football coach
f) We don't know. He ran away.

4. The game of basketball was invented by

a) James A. Naismith
b) A group of basket weavers
c) A very lonely tall man
d) A famous shoe company
e) The NBA

parents tell their children. His was the classic Cinderella story—from lowly shepherd boy to soldier to sovereign king. He had made it to the top. And as if all that wasn't enough, he was also a man of character, a man of God.

He was King David.

But all that changed one spring evening. Good King David made a choice that would forever change his life and future.

Look at 2 Samuel 11:1-4 in your Bible. After reading the passage, write down the choices you see David making.

Verse 1, he made the choice to
Verse 2, he made the choice to
Verse 3, he made the choice to
Verse 4, he made the choice to

We're used to thinking that David made his royal blunder when he chose to commit adultery with Bathsheba. But where do you think his downfall began, and why?

What seemed to be an insignificant choice turned out to be a huge mistake in David's life. Who would have thought that staying at home when all the other kings were in battle would have been such a big deal? David learned the hard way that life is a series of choices, all somehow linked to one another. Like dominoes, each choice we make begins a chain reaction of other choices and circumstances. Sometimes those small choices can bring about devastating consequences. A bad choice may begin innocently enough, but it can lead to more than we bargained for. It's like the saying:

> Sin will always take you farther than you want to go, make you stay longer than you want to stay, and cost you more than you want to pay.

Think of how many people's lives have been changed by what at the time appeared to be a small choice to

- have one more beer.
- dive into shallow water.
- try cocaine "just once."
- get into the backseat.
- shoplift.
- go for a short joyride.

If you're not careful, a small choice can turn into a big mistake. Has that ever happened to you?

Once I made the choice to _____

and that led to _____

I must pay attention to the little choices I make because every decision is important and has consequences.

By the way, here are the answers to the multiple-choice quiz: 1. h or i; 2. (Excuse me?); 3. a; 4. a

The Ripple Effect

The Choice

When I was in college, I had a crush on a girl for a while. She wasn't your ordinary girl. This girl was unbelievably good-looking. Anyway, once on a retreat with some friends, we decided to play a game where the girls blindfolded the guys and led them around the camp. This exercise was supposed to teach us to have faith in other people. Fortunately for me, I was able to choose my crush as my partner. I was, to put it mildly, extremely excited. So the blindfolds were put on, and Miss Wonderful took me by her sweet little hand and began to lead me around the camp into telephone poles, trees, cars, walls, ditches, other people, and even down stairs. By the time it was over, I had bumps, cuts, and bruises all over. Oh, I learned something about trust all right, or rather about how not to trust someone. For some reason, our relationship never blossomed after that. I guess I chose the wrong partner, and for the wrong reason.

Like my experience, wrong choices can blind you to what's really true in life. When you make wrong choices, you lose the ability to see things the way they really are. You end up being led around by your wrong choices. Take relationships, for example. Have you ever wondered why everyone except Jenn can clearly see that Chris is a total loser and bad news for her? Jenn's poor choice for a boyfriend has blinded her to the truth. It's the same reason why an addict has trouble admitting he has a drug problem. His choices have blinded him to the truth.

God has given you freedom to make your own choices, but unfortunately you do not have the freedom to determine the outcome of those choices. Making choices is like throwing a rock into a lake and watching the ripple effect it causes. One rock produces many ripples.

Staying home seemed innocent enough for David. One look at Bathsheba couldn't harm anyone. Having her only visit the royal palace wouldn't be wrong. Just one little act of adultery wouldn't hurt anybody. After all, David was the king. Nothing could happen to him.

Keep reading in 2 Samuel, and see the consequences of David's wrong choices.

> 2 Samuel 11:5
>
> Consequence 1

In an attempt to try and cover up his sin, what other sins did David end up committing? (vv. 7-15, 24)

> 2 Samuel 12:7-8
>
> Consequence 2

Think of all the great benefits and blessings God had planned for David.

> 2 Samuel 12:10-12
>
> Consequence 3

You can read this unbelievable story in 2 Samuel 13—18.

> 2 Samuel 12:14-18
>
> Consequence 4

As if all his other heartaches weren't enough! This was a tragic consequence!

Just one small choice, right?

David confessed and repented of his sin and was completely forgiven and restored to fellowship with God (2 Samuel 12:13; Psalm 51; Psalm 32). He is still the only man in the Bible who is described as "a man after [God's] own heart" (Acts 13:22). But David could not escape the awful consequences of his bad choices.

Several years ago, Michael Jackson came to Houston to do a concert at the Summit Arena. A friend of mine promised my brother and me that he could get us the best seats in the house, and we jumped at the chance. Arriving at the Summit just before the concert, my friend led us past all the normal gate entrances. *Wow, these must be really great seats,* we thought. Then he took us up a flight of stairs, up another flight of stairs, up a ladder, and finally onto a catwalk that stretched right over the top of where Michael was moonwalking.

Things were cool for us, until the security showed up. Apparently, they didn't take too kindly to our bird's-eye view of Mr. Jackson. In a matter of minutes, we were handcuffed and escorted outside. I was trying to think of what I was going to say to my dad in my one phone call from jail. Right before we were put into the squad car, a policeman, who was a member of our church, recognized us and allowed us to go free. Relieved, we learned an incredible lesson about choices and consequences.

Have you thought about the possible consequences in the choices you make or will make in the near future? Considering the possible consequences of your choices, what would you do in the following situations?

- *You're at a party and someone brings in the beer. Everyone starts drinking. What do you do?*
- *You're out with your friends and they all want to go to a certain movie, but you're not sure if your parents (or God) would approve. What do you do?*
- *You're on your first date with that special person. At the end of the evening, he or she wants to make out. What do you do?*
- *You're over at a friend's house and he brings out a pornographic magazine. What do you do?*

According to Galatians 6:7, why is considering the consequences of your choices so important?

I must consider the consequences of my choices before I make them.

Choosing to Win

The Choice

As a boy, he decided to pick up a basketball instead of a trumpet. When he was cut by his high-school basketball team, he chose not to give up or quit. When the offers started pouring in for college scholarships, he chose to attend the University of North Carolina. He decided to sign with the Chicago Bulls and to stay with one team. Today, instead of Michael Jordan, insurance salesman, or Michael Jordan, automotive mechanic, or Michael Jordan, trumpet player, it's Michael Jordan—superstar, household name, movie star, scoring champ, the greatest basketball player who ever lived. We can trace his monumental success back to one small decision to pick up a basketball. One choice led to another, and a chain of events resulted that has thrilled the heart of every basketball fan in the world!

Have you ever thought about the great things God has planned for you? It makes sense that you should want to be great for him, too. Well, your daily choices are the road that will take you there. Many times you make good choices in life that turn into great victories. For example, the choice to

- date and marry the right person
- attend a decent college
- go on a summer missions trip
- trust Jesus as your Savior

Those are all great decisions, all life-changing choices. But how can you make the right choices each day? What should you do when you're facing tough choices? Here are four fantastic principles to help you make those daily decisions:

1. Pray about your choices.

What promise does God make to you in James 1:5?

2. Ask godly people what they think.

What does God guarantee when you do this? (Proverbs 11:14)

Whose godly counsel would you seek?

3. Consult your Bible.

In what way will God's Word help you? (Psalm 119:105)

When Christmas or birthdays come around, do you ever wonder what to give your friends or family? A catalog recently featured a unique gift for the person who has everything: house slippers. But these house slippers weren't your average under-the-bed slippers. These slippers had headlights—rather, "toe" lights! Every time you walked, little flashlights in the toes would light up. I guess this gift would especially come in handy if you walk around your house in the dark. As strange as this gift sounds, it illustrates exactly what the Bible does for you. It lights your path as you walk around in a dark world. Look for guidance in your Bible.

4. Learn from past mistakes.

To what does Solomon compare repeating the same mistake over and over? (Proverbs 26:11 and yuck!)

Of course, if you have serious reservations about a decision, then it's usually best to "play it safe." A good rule of thumb is: When in doubt, throw it out.

Here are some critical decision areas Christian students say they face. Circle the ones that you confront the most, and add some of your own.

Dating	Drugs	Relationships
Morality	Drinking	Sex
Time	Church	Bible study
Prayer	Speech	

What is the one area where you probably will need to make a choice this week?

Put the four principles into action the next time you have a decision to make!

TAKE-AWAY THOUGHT · *As I make choices, I can depend on the wisdom from God's Word to guide me.*

Aiming to Please

The Choice

Grandpa had his two grandchildren on his lap one evening, telling them a bedtime story. "Yep, I'll never forget the time I was hunting deer in the deep woods one day when all of a sudden a huge twelve-foot tall grizzly bear was standing right in front of me. Growling and pawing at the air, he showed his long, white, razor-sharp fangs."

The two grandchildren were wide-eyed at this point as their grandfather continued. "Why, I was so scared I dropped my gun and made a run for it, but I could hear the bear right behind me breathing down my neck. I kept looking for some way to escape when I spotted a tree limb straight ahead. The only problem was that the limb was way too high—some twenty feet off the ground. But I had no choice but to try and jump for it. It was my only chance. By this time the bear had his mouth open, ready to swallow me up in one bite, when I gave everything I had and jumped for the limb."

"Grandpa, Grandpa, did you make it? Did you?" asked the two children.

Shaking his head, the old-timer replied, "No, my darlings. I'm afraid I missed it—but I did catch it on the way down!"

You could safely say that old Granddad had a little motivation to catch the limb. That little story points out that motivation is everything when you're attempting something important. If you want to show the world how God lives in you, then your motivation is pretty significant.

A person's motivation is simply why that person does what he or she does. For example, what do you think motivates someone to

- run for student government?
- make good grades?
- play on the team?
- get a part-time job?
- want to be popular?
- get a driver's license?
- buy a new outfit?
- go to college?
- run away from home?
- shoplift?

When I was a boy, I got a Cub Scout knife as a gift. Wanting to prove to my brother how cool it was, I took him into the bathroom, locked the door, and got a can of my dad's shaving cream. I opened the knife to the pointy blade and poked the bottom of the can to prove just how sharp the point was. Dumb move. Shaving cream sprayed everywhere—on the floor, on the walls, on the ceiling, on the mirror. We jumped into the shower and pulled the curtain as the can kept spraying.

By this time my dad was at the door, shouting and wondering what in the world was going on in there. The door was locked, so he couldn't get in, and we weren't about to come out. Finally, we devised a plan. We would let the can spray into the toilet until the shaving cream ran out. Great idea, right? Wrong. We couldn't flush the toilet fast enough, so my brother tried to push the shaving cream down! He ended up getting his hand stuck in the toilet. Needless to say, I learned a valuable lesson about trying to impress other people.

It all comes down to why you do what you do. Whether good or bad, all of your actions have motivations behind them. And the same is true in your Christian life.

Read Ephesians 5:10. What should be our number-one motivation in life?

This sounds simple, but what does it really mean? Put the verse in your own words.

If you think about it, everybody is trying to please someone. Complete these sentences.

- A student tries to please his _____
- A player tries to please her _____
- A child tries to please his _____
- An employee tries to please her _____
- A band member tries to please her _____
- A Christian tries to please his _____

Can you think of anyone else you try to please other than the Lord?

Check off all the reasons why you want to please others.

- to be recognized ___
- to be accepted ___
- to be rewarded ___
- to feel good about yourself ___
- to be liked ___
- to be popular ___
- to avoid punishment ___
- all of the above ___

Have you ever thought about why you do what you do as a Christian? Ever examined your motivation for doing the things that Christians are supposed to do? Why do you read your Bible? go to church? pray? live a godly lifestyle? witness to others?

Ephesians 5:10 talks about finding out what pleases God. In your opinion, what pleases God the most?

What motivates you to want to please God in your life?

TAKE-AWAY THOUGHT

In order to live a life that's different, I must seek to please God in all I do.

CHAPTER EIGHT

If You Believe in Miracles

When you're far
Far from the light
Feel there's no hope
Left in sight
And the answer can't be found
It's no secret
I'm telling you now

Just hold on
'Cause it's gonna come
If you just pray to the One
Who hears your every cry
Don't give up on life

Chorus:
If you believe in miracles now
We can change the world around
It all begins with one
That's how the battle's won
It's time to believe
If you need a miracle now
You can change your world around
Have faith enough to see
How great His love can be
It's time to believe
(In miracles)

If your heart
Is driven by fear
Your road will be short and unclear
Just take what's left inside
His love won't be denied

[repeat chorus]

There's Always Hope

Miracles

It has been said that a person can survive 8 days without water, 40 days without food, 8 minutes without air—but he can't live one minute without hope.

When people have no hope, they have no reason to go on. They simply give up on life and surrender in defeat. Many times people lose hope when

- the doctor says the cancer is terminal.
- Mom and Dad say the marriage is over.
- the coach says their playing days are over.
- they look in the mirror and see things they can't change.
- they can't break free from their sadness.
- they commit the same sin over and over again.
- they can't foresee things ever getting any better.

Take heart. God is a God of hope. Many times in Scripture he communicated hope to his children through miracles. What do you think is the greatest miracle God has ever done?

- Creation
- The creation of man
- The Flood
- The ten plagues
- Parting the Red Sea

- Joshua and the walls of Jericho
- Jesus' virgin birth
- Turning water into wine
- Multiplying the fish and loaves
- Healing the sick
- Raising Lazarus from the dead
- Making a paralyzed man walk
- The Resurrection

Why did you choose that particular miracle?

When he walked on the earth, Jesus performed many miracles—both in nature and in man. Each miracle he did was sort of a miniportrait of who he was. Every miracle told a story about what God was like. But no miracle—past, present, or future—compares with the one he does in a person's life when he saves that person from sin and makes him or her a new creation. Salvation is the greatest miracle of all.

In John 4, Jesus has an encounter with a Samaritan woman. As the story unfolds, we see how Christ brings a desperately needed miracle into this needy woman's life—a miracle he still performs today.

Turn to John 4 and read verses 1-5. Back in Jesus' day, there were no Jeeps or minivans. Only four-wheel-drive donkeys (with just one air bag!). Jesus didn't even have one of those. He traveled the old-fashioned way—on foot.

What do you discover about Jesus in verse 6?

Jesus was traveling from Judea (in the south) to Galilee (in the north), a distance somewhere between twenty and thirty miles. No wonder Jesus was tired. Right in the middle of these two regions is Samaria. But no self-respecting Jew would have stopped in Samaria, no matter how tired he was. The Jews and Samaritans hated each other. To avoid going through Samaria, the Jews normally took one of two roads that bypassed this region. But Jesus was no ordinary man.

So Jesus is worn out from his walk. What would you be interested in doing if you had walked that far in the blazing desert sun?

Choke down a burger and Coke, then crash in bed, right? Not Jesus. He has an appointment to keep—a divine appointment. Only the person he's meeting at the well doesn't realize she's about to have a face-to-face encounter with the God who made her.

> Jesus is hanging out at the well while his disciples go into town to get some food. While he is there, who happens to come along?

> What does Jesus ask her? (v. 7)

> How does she react to this request? (v. 9)

> Why? (v. 9)

In his day, Jesus redefined the meaning of love, kindness, and mercy. Because of this, he became politically incorrect to the religious establishment and even surprised his own disciples. A lot of racial tension existed between the Jews and Samaritans, but Jesus crossed regional, racial, and religious barriers just to speak to this woman.

> Now read vv. 10-14. Though Jesus has asked her for a drink of water, he now offers her something. What is it?

What is the difference between the "well" she speaks of in verse 11 and the "well" Jesus talks about in verse 14? See how many differences you can think of.

Her Well   His Well

What do you think Jesus meant when he said that she would never thirst again?

Obviously, that is one of the benefits of becoming a Christian. Why not pause here and write down as many benefits of being a Christian as you can think of. Thank God for each one of them as you write.

TAKE-AWAY THOUGHT **Jesus offers me a relationship that is extremely hip and that truly satisfies.**

Living H₂O **DAY 32**
Miracles

Ｗhile traveling to Oklahoma to speak at a youth camp, my wife and I were driving on a lonely stretch of country road, a very lonely stretch. My wife insisted we were lost; I was confident we weren't because I had the map. Intricately drawn by the camp director, this map detailed just about every bend and turn in southern Oklahoma. He had even included landmarks, stop signs, and farmhouses. We continued driving on into the night until we reached the dead end of a dirt road. When the dust settled, I squinted through the darkness to see that on my left was a herd of cows in a pasture staring at me with puzzled looks on their faces. On my right was my wife with a similar look on her face. Only hers had a hint of "I told you so" sprinkled in there as well. With a gentle whisper, she asked if I might be willing to check the map one more time, which at this point I was more than happy to do. As I did this, I discovered to my surprise that I had been reading the map upside down for a while.

The blow to my male ego was so great that I had to relinquish my job as trip navigator for the rest of the way. My wife has been taking care of the maps ever since.

In John 4, Jesus laid out for the Samaritan a sort of spiritual road map. Because he knew which side was up, he led her straight to forgiveness and salvation without any detours or mishaps.

Open your Bible to John 4. Before this woman could experience her personal miracle, Jesus helped her realize something. What was it? (vv. 15-18)

Do you have any idea why Christ wanted her to admit this? (See also Romans 3:23; 1 John 1:9.)

Jesus brought to the surface the worst thing about her. Through his miraculous insight, she discovered that

- he knew everything about her and her sin, yet he loved her.
- she had to admit her sin in order to be forgiven and experience salvation.

There is no salvation without repentance and confession. God is a holy God and cannot allow sin in his presence (Habakkuk 1:13). In fact, he is righteous and must punish sin (Romans 6:23). But because he loves us, he has provided a way out of that judgment (John 3:16-17; Romans 5:8-9).

As a result of their conversation so far, what did this woman come to realize about Jesus? (v. 19)

The woman had a religious issue to discuss with him. She wanted to know the proper place to worship God (v. 20). Jesus told her that where you worship was not nearly as important as who you worship (vv. 21-24).

What else does Jesus tell her? (v. 26)

Jesus and the Samaritan woman have talked about living water, her sinful past and present, worship, salvation, and finally the Messiah. About this time, Jesus' disciples walk up. Read verse 27.

How do you think the woman felt about Jesus? about the disciples?

There are four basic life needs:

- Air
- Water
- Bread (food)
- Light

Have you ever noticed that Jesus meets all of those needs?

- Air—He gives us spiritual life through the breath of the Spirit (John 3:8).
- Water—He gives us living water (John 4:14).
- Bread—He is the bread of life (John 6:48).
- Light—He is the light of the world (John 8:12).

How has Jesus met these needs in your life? List some of the ways Jesus has provided for you, both physically and spiritually.

Jesus satisfies me and meets my every need.

Stairway to Heaven

Miracles

In the Wild West, the Winchester rifle was used by more cowboys, outlaws, and lawmen than any other rifle in the 1800s. As a result, the Winchester family made quite a fortune. Mrs. Sarah Winchester consulted a psychic (with the psychic hotline, of course—not!) who told her that her family's rifles had brought a curse on her that would haunt her for the rest of her life. To escape the curse, Mrs. Winchester decided to turn her San Jose, California, farmhouse into a mansion. She hired workers to work on her house every day until she died in 1922. Her plan was to confuse the ghosts of those killed by her husband's rifles. She had builders make doors open into walls, construct stairs that led to nowhere, and create secret passageways and upside-down pillars and posts. Because of the constant building, this house going nowhere ended up with 13 bathrooms, 52 skylights, 47 fireplaces, 10,000 windows, 40 staircases, and 2,000 doorways.

A lot of people's lives are like that house—confusing, unplanned, and going nowhere. Eventually this type of lifestyle leads to a dead end. If your life has direction, meaning, and purpose, then others will want what you have. It's like the old proverb that says, "What's in the well comes up in the bucket." In other words, what a person is really like on the inside will come out in his or her life sooner or later. Apparently the woman at the well knew enough to trust in Christ for salvation, because she immediately ran into town to tell everyone about him. She went to the well to fill her water jug and left with the whole well—a well of living water!

Look at John 4:28. Who were the first people she told about her encounter with Christ?

What did she tell them? (v. 29)

Now read verses 30 and 39. What happened as a result of her testimony?

Imagine how hopeless this woman felt. She had been through five marriages, and the man she was living with wasn't even her husband. She had the worst reputation of anyone in town. No one respected her, especially the men who said they loved her. Her life was ruined.

And yet on a routine trip to the town well, her path crossed with Jesus'. He came to her town just to meet her. He pointed out her sin, and he also offered her the cure for her condition. He offered hope for her life. He offered her cleansing from her past, forgiveness for her sins, satisfaction for her soul. He could have given her a supernatural sign. He could have changed the water into wine. But instead, the miracle he performed was not inside the well, but inside of her. He offered her the miracle of salvation. And she accepted it. Because of him, her lifestyle, reputation, and destiny were changed forever! Her life was made new, and even though she didn't know much about him, she told everyone what she did know about her new Savior.

As we track this woman's growing knowledge of who Christ was, we see her understanding of him growing. She went from seeing him as a

- man to a
- Jew to
- one greater than Jacob to a
- prophet to the
- Messiah to her
- Savior

> Long ago, there was an Italian general named Garibaldi. Once, while at war, the general's men camped on a sheep farm. Through a careless prank, one of the young sheep was let out of the gate and got lost. The general felt so bad about it that he organized his men to look for the lost sheep. Long into the night they searched, but no sheep. Finally, the general called off the search. At dawn, the general's aide came to his tent to waken him for breakfast. When he opened the flap of the tent, he saw Garibaldi asleep on his cot—but something else caught his eye. Next to the general was the little lost lamb, snuggled up to him. The aide realized that, after Garibaldi had sent his men to bed, he had spent the rest of the night looking for the lost sheep until he found it.

That's exactly the way God is with you and me. That's how much he loved this woman.

Who is Jesus to you today? Is he just a figure in history, or is he your personal Savior? Have you experienced the miracle of salvation in your life? Why not take a few minutes and write a thank-you note to the Lord, telling him how grateful you are for your salvation.

Dear Master,

I want to thank you for

With much love and gratitude,

Your child

As long as Christ offers the miracle of salvation, no one is beyond hope. Why not bring a friend to the well of living water? Maybe you could be used by God to introduce a friend to a miracle today.

Remember, as long as there's Jesus, there's hope. So join the "3-H Club": happiness, hope, and heaven.

TAKE-AWAY THOUGHT

Through Jesus, I find my way to happiness, hope, and heaven.

Airborne Believer

Miracles

This was a big mistake, I thought. I looked around my high-school chemistry class only to see National Merit finalists sitting in the desks around me. It was one of *those* classes, and something told me I didn't belong. My guidance counselor had suggested I take the class. But my experience in science was limited to making smoke bombs with the chemistry set I had gotten for Christmas one year. Still, I thought it would be fun. And besides, my good friend Greg was taking this class, so I signed up.

What a bonehead move.

Foreign charts with strange symbols decorated the walls. They may as well have been written in Latin, because I sure couldn't understand them (now that I think about it, they *were* written in Latin!). I thought my teacher would be like the Professor from *Gilligan's Island* and we would have tons of fun. Instead, he turned out to be an old college professor who had decided to finish out his career tormenting teenagers with chemical equations. I needed an interpreter when he spoke. Everyone seemed to be breezing through the material—everyone but me. I just couldn't understand the concepts. It was like trying to nail Jell-O to the wall. The final straw came when we got back the results from our first exam. Let's put it this way, when you don't even score your shoe size, it's time to drop back and punt.

I punted.

Sometimes overcoming a difficult past is a bit like that chemistry class. You feel like you're behind and will never catch up. How can God give you hope when you're under the pile? It's through his power working in you. Today in Isaiah 40, you will learn that he is there to provide the power and strength to do what you could never do on your own—get through impossible circumstances.

Read Isaiah 40:28. How does Isaiah describe the Lord in this verse?

This means God is eternal and unchanging. His power for you is everlasting. The word LORD in Hebrew is *Yahweh,* which is the personal name of God. His power for you is personal.

He is the all-powerful Creator and ruler of all. His power for you is unlimited. Put those together in your mind:

- Everlasting
- Personal
- Unlimited

How much more power could you want? Isaiah goes on to say that this God never gets tired of helping you. In fact, he actually delights in helping you! But that's not all. Look at verse 29.

Who does he give strength to?

For whom does he increase power?

Does that describe you? Do you qualify to receive God's strength?

Read on. Verse 30 reminds us that even the strongest believers grow tired in the battle. That means everybody. But Isaiah encourages us to "wait on the Lord" (v. 31). This means to "lean heavily on," "trust in," or "look to."

If you do this, what does God promise you? (v. 31)

This means you exchange your tired, worn-out strength for a renewed strength. It's like trading in an old, broken-down car for a brand-new one. That's a pretty good trade. That's what you really need when you face problems!

What is the result of leaning on his strength during those times? (v. 31)

Have you ever realized that

- an eagle sees the earth, but is not weighed down by it or entangled in it?
- an eagle rarely uses its wings, but effortlessly glides and soars through the air? He has learned to depend on the wind for his lift.

The same is true for you when you depend on God's power. You can see your problems without being dragged down by them. You can soar above your circumstances. You do this every time you give him your tired spirit, worries, fears, anxieties, burdens, troubles, and problems. The result is that you will overcome life, rather than letting life overcome you.

God's power is sufficient for your needs and more (check Ephesians 3:20-21).

God is willing and able to give you his power, and even more strength than you need, ask for, or imagine. It would be like your mother asking you to go to the supermarket to buy a loaf of bread, then giving you a one-hundred-dollar bill to buy it. That's more than enough. God gives you plenty of strength—all you need.

What's wrong with relying on your own strength?
Why is God's strength better?
What do you need his power for this week?
Rely on and trust in God's strength right now, and you will start soaring above your problems just as the eagle does.

By depending on God's strength, I can live above my circumstances.

CHAPTER NINE

Love Wants Nothing

I've seen the hand of pride reach out
To feed the hunger of my doubt
Disguised as an old familiar friend
It promises to lead me on
To meet my need and make me strong
And tells me it won't break me if I'll bend

But I've been through that lie before
Seen what lies behind that door
And what it costs is more than I could pay

Chorus:
Love wants nothing
Love gives everything
Love wants nothing
It's the power of a man with the bread in his hands
The fulfilling of every need
(It's the heart of a man with his head in his hand)
The fulfilling of every dream

I have prayed thy will be done
Even said thy kingdom come
But often seemed to walk away unchanged
Heard the roar of my own will
Drowning out all else
All that I believed was rearranged

But I've been through that lie before
Seen what lies behind the door
And what it takes is more than I can give

Been through all those lies before
Somewhere's so much more

[repeat chorus]

A Love That Won't Let Go

Love Wants Nothing

One Christmas Eve, I was in Starkeville, Mississippi, at my brother's house. During the night, my brother's wife got really sick. In fact, she was so sick that we decided to take her to a doctor in Jackson. Because of the long drive, I decided to fly her there in my plane. Hopping on board, we took off. When we got near Jackson, it was almost entirely covered in fog. No problem—the air-traffic controller would guide me in safely. The air-traffic controller and I talked for some time until I finally spotted the runway on my own. As soon as I landed, I knew something was wrong. There were no other airplanes around. I had landed at an old abandoned airfield instead of the Jackson airport! I later discovered that the air-traffic controller had been talking to another plane the entire time, and I thought he was talking to me.

Whether intentionally or by mistake, sometimes as Christians we can get foggy about the important things and end up doing the opposite of what we originally planned. We can get so caught up in doing things *for* God that we lose sight of our relationship *with* him. Our relationship with Christ deteriorates into mere religion. Our devotion becomes a duty. Instead of prayer being a conversation, it becomes a chore.

Have you ever felt like that?

When this happens, we need to take a step back to see the big picture of our relationship with our heavenly Father. There is no better way to do that than to remind ourselves of how much God truly loves us. Over the next few days, you will discover the wonderful love of God. When you've finished, I hope you will be aware of many unbelievable ways God loves you.

How is God's love for you described in Psalm 103:11?

The general definition of *love* in Hebrew (one of the languages the Bible was written in) is a "loyal, faithful *love*." God's great love for you in this verse is illustrated by the distance between the heavens and the earth. Have you ever thought about how far the heavens are from the earth?

The moon is 252,000 miles from the earth. If you started walking today and walked 24 miles a day, it would take you only about 29 years to get there (encouraging, huh?). But if walking sounds boring to you, how about traveling at the speed of light? Moving at 186,000 miles per second, you could get to the moon in less than two seconds and make Mercury in four and a half minutes. You would arrive at Jupiter in the time it takes to go through this devotion and get to Saturn in an hour and ten minutes. That's not bad for a trip of 793 million miles—but talk about jet lag!

As David looked up at the stars and thought about how great God's love is, it must have blown his mind (as it does ours) to think of how far away the heavens are from the earth. He compared the vast distance of space (infinity) to God's love for him. Have you ever looked up at the stars and considered how vast outer space is?

No matter how many times you look up at the stars, you will never see them all. That's exactly how it is with God's love for you.

> **Before I asked my wife to marry me, I went to a jewelry store to pick out a ring. The jeweler brought out a beautiful diamond and placed it on a black velvet background to highlight the color and brilliance of the precious stone. Then he placed it under a magnifier and began showing me the many different facets of this gorgeous stone. Each time he rotated it, I gained a new appreciation for its beauty. Then he dropped the bombshell by revealing how much this rock was going to cost me. The next thing I remember is hearing the paramedics say, "Sir, are you all right? Wake up!"**

(OK, that part didn't really happen, but I did feel like passing out.) Though it was a very costly stone, it didn't matter. It was well worth the price for my sweetheart (a very righteous fox).

Every time you look at God's love for you as demonstrated at the Cross, you will see a precious diamond whose beauty you can never fully explore. Each time you pause to gaze at his love, you will see something new and be awestruck by how vast it is.

Write out a short prayer from your heart, asking God to give you eyes to see the depth of his love for you.

TAKE-AWAY THOUGHT **God's love for me is totally faithful and infinite.**

Getting What You Don't Deserve

Love Wants Nothing

*B*ack in 1954, a milk-shake-mixer salesman named Ray Kroc walked into a family-owned restaurant in San Bernardino, California, expecting to make a sale. The restaurant already owned eight of his mixers, but Ray wasn't there to sell them another machine. He was there to sell an idea. Ray, who was very impressed with the speed and efficiency of the little restaurant, wanted to talk to the owners about starting a franchise. Convinced it would be a good deal, the owners agreed. The very first restaurant in the chain opened the following year in Des Plaines, Illinois. Five years, 228 stores, and forty million dollars later, *McDonald's* had become a household name.

Do you ever wonder how things got started?

- Where did bubblegum come from?
- Who invented dental floss?
- When did people first eat pizza?
- Who built the first bridge?
- When did Americans first start paying taxes?
- Where did blue jeans come from?

All these are questions you are dying to have answered, right? Not. Well here's a much better question: When do you think God first began loving you? Now that's a good question. You can find the answer in Ephesians 1:4-5.

From these verses, when do you think God first began loving you?

God tells us that it was sometime before the earth was created—sometime in eternity past. It could have been a hundred thousand years ago or a hundred million years ago. Or it could even be that he has always loved you for all eternity.

How do you think God could love you before you existed? (This is a true "brain buster.")

Like God himself, his love for you never had a beginning (and it doesn't have an end, either). But there's something else about God's love you need to know.

Since you're already in Ephesians, look over at chapter 2, verses 1-3. Here Paul gives a biographical sketch of all believers' lives before they came to know Christ. From these verses, write down what was true about you before you became a Christian.

- I was (v. 1)

- I followed (v. 2)

- I lived to (v. 3)

- I was, by nature, (v. 3)

Pretty bleak picture, huh? Yet it is an accurate one. Remember Romans 5:8?

But God showed his great love for us by sending Christ to die for us while we were still sinners.

What does that say about God's love for you?

There is nothing you could ever do to make yourself worthy of God's love. That's because his love was never meant to be earned. It was only meant to be received.

Do you remember the story of the Prodigal Son? One brother wanted to get his inheritance early instead of waiting until the proper time. Reluctantly, his father agreed. So, leaving home, the young man went away to seek the pleasures of the world. But after a while, all his money was gone, and so was his happiness. He had ruined his reputation, sinned against God and his father, and disgraced the family name. Financially broke and broken spiritually, he returned to his father's house hoping to become a servant.

All along his dad had been praying and waiting. Seeing his son from a distance, the father ran to meet him, kissing him and weeping. Though the son certainly didn't deserve to be welcomed back, he was. Though he didn't deserve to be a part of the family again, he was. Though he certainly didn't deserve a party, he got one. The father's love for his son was undeserved love.

Even though we don't deserve God's love, like that son, we are embraced and loved anyway. Don't forget—God loved you before you were born. He loved you even when you were lost and full of sin. He loves you during the times you wander away from him. You can never do anything to deserve his love. Just enjoy it and appreciate it.

How does God's lavish, forgiving love make you feel?

What difference does this love make in your daily relationship with him?

God loves me even though I don't deserve it.

A cold drink. A hot bath. A happy reunion. Christmas morning. A home run. An A-plus. A loving family. Sleep. Playing in the snow. A warm fire. Friday nights. Lying out in the sun. Body surfing. A crisp red apple. A juicy hamburger. Friends. Getting out of school for the summer. Hearing your parents say yes. A sunny day. A great movie. Loud music. Group photos. A college acceptance letter. School is canceled. Getting your braces off. Cookies and cold milk. Spring break. Your first car. Returning home after a long trip.

What do all these things have in common? They are all some of the good things we enjoy. They bring us a sense of satisfaction and contentment. Too many times, we focus on the disappointments in life. We've all had setbacks, but we need to look for more of those good things. If you stop long enough to look around you, you'll find many good things God sends your way.

Stop right now and think of at least five really good things that have happened to you in the past two weeks. Write them down here.

1.

2.

3.

4.

5.

Now let's take this a little further and think of something that's even better—the love of God.

Look up Psalm 63:3-5. How is God's love described in verse 3?

What do you think that means?

In what ways would you say God's love is better than all the good things we've been talking about?

What does David say he will do as a result of God's love? (vv. 3-4)

> **Imagine it's dinnertime and you're famished. Sitting at the table, to your delight you discover your mom has prepared your favorite food. You can't believe it. You haven't eaten all day, and you savor every bite. It tastes great. Your mom has never cooked such a meal. While you're enjoying this, thinking about how she ought to open a restaurant or something, she comes in from the kitchen with your all-time favorite dessert. You can't believe it. You pinch yourself to make sure you're not dreaming. You wonder if you have any more room for food, but those thoughts quickly pass. Afterward, you can hardly move, so you waddle over to the couch and crash just in time to see your favorite TV show. At this point, your dad walks over and asks if you'd like anything else to eat. And you respond, "No thanks, Dad. I'm _____!"**

Now we all know what goes in that blank, don't we? The reason you can't eat any more is that your hunger has been totally, completely, and thoroughly satisfied. You're full. Stuffed, right? What a great feeling!

What your body feels after that kind of meal is exactly what your soul feels when you understand and experience God's love each day. His love satisfies. It fills you up. When you know you are loved by him, you don't want what the world has to offer. You're fulfilled. And since you're already full of your soul's favorite food, why would you want the rotten vegetables the world offers you?

However, when you're really hungry, any old food will do, won't it? The same thing happens spiritually. We often go through the spiritual drive-up window and fill our hearts with spiritual junk food. Look at the list below, and highlight some of the spiritual junk food you settle for at times.

- Wrong friends
- Popularity
- Fun
- Self-reliance
- Romance
- Laughter
- Retreating to your room
- Working out
- Getting mad
-
-

None of these things can satisfy the hunger of your soul. They only make you feel full for a short while. But soon the gnawing hunger pangs for love come right back. Psalm 34:8 says "Taste and see that the Lord is good." The more you feed your soul on his love, the more you will be satisfied and spiritually full. So when you find yourself hungry for something to eat, don't settle for the world's junk food and the devil's leftovers. Let God bring to you the greatest spiritual food, the best of all—his enjoyable love that is guaranteed to please you and satisfy your spirit.

God's love satisfies and fulfills me like nothing else can.

A Priceless Masterpiece

L o v e   W a n t s   N o t h i n g

Several years ago, one of the richest men in America was sitting alone in his mansion. Nestled in the mountains and secluded from the rest of the world, this man had everything he wanted that money could buy. Thumbing through an art dealer magazine that evening, he spotted a beautiful painting. It was a very old portrait by a famous artist, and it cost several hundred thousand dollars. At once, he called his buyer and told him to call and ask about the painting. When the buyer called the art dealer, he was saddened to discover it had already been sold.

The buyer returned to the rich man and told him what had happened. Outraged, the billionaire ordered his buyer to get on a plane and search the ends of the earth until he found that painting. "I want that portrait!" he screamed. The buyer began his search. After several months, he had come up with nothing. The painting was simply nowhere to be found.

Returning to the mansion late at night, the buyer knew he would be fired in the morning. But before going to bed, a thought popped into his mind. Walking over to the vast storage building the billionaire had built to house all his treasures, the buyer began to sort through all the hundreds of paintings the man owned. About an hour later—bingo! There it was. This wealthy man had owned the priceless work of art all along.

When God thinks of valuable treasures, what do you suppose comes to his mind? What work of art is priceless to him? Wouldn't it be great if God would just tell you the answer to those questions? Wouldn't it be cool if he could speak to you right now?

The good news is that you can hear him speak to you from his Word. Your Bible is God's heart and mind. Through it, you can know the real truth about how valuable you are to God.

Today, you'll investigate three truths about your relationship with God.

Truth 1—God Made You (Psalm 139:13-16)

What can you discover in these verses about how God made you?

We identify people today by the labels they wear. Nike, Reebok, Gap, Polo, etc. But the Bible says that you have been designed by God himself. You bear his image in you. He was personally involved in handcrafting you. There's no one else like you. You're an original!

Truth 2—God Knows You (Psalm 139:1-6, 17-18)

What does God know about you?

According to verses 17-18, how many times does God think about you?

Next time you're at the beach, reach down and pick up a pinch of sand between your fingers. Count those grains of sand (if you can). Then look down the beach and try to calculate all the grains of sand on that beach. Then multiply that number by all the grains on all the beaches of the world. Then throw into your calculation all the sand in the deserts of the world. Verse 18 says God's thoughts about you outnumber that!

Truth 3—God Cares for You (Romans 5:8; 1 Peter 1:17-19)

Just how much does God care about you?

How did he demonstrate that love and prove it to you?

Imagine you are a slave and that you are being sold at an auction. Someone steps forward and offers $2.19 for you. How does that make you feel?

But suppose a stranger in the back of the crowd makes another offer and gets into a bidding war with someone else. The price begins to rise. Fifty dollars. Then one hundred. Four hundred. One thousand. After a long pause, the person in the back comes forward. You can see by his face that he is a kind and benevolent person. Approaching the auction block, he reaches into his satchel and produces a bag full of cash, jewelry, and silver and gold coins. He places the bag containing this fortune on the auction block and says, "This is all the wealth I have in the world. I want to purchase this slave and set him free."

Now how do you feel?

God had at his disposal all the money and gold and silver ever made, combined with the planets, stars, and galaxies, but turned to something even more valuable—his own dear Son—to give in exchange for your salvation and freedom from sin. God thinks you're worth that much!

All this adds up to the fact that God made you, thinks about you constantly, and cares deeply for you.

Your value and worth are not dependent on your

- beauty
- wealth
- intelligence
- popularity
- personality
- talents

You are valuable just as you are, just as God made you. You have worth because Jesus Christ made you, knows you, died for you, and cares about you. You are priceless to him.

Once there was a famous painter named Velázquez who painted a portrait called "The Portrait of Juan de Pareja." When this painting was sold, someone paid $5,554,000 for it! The person who bought it paid such a high price

not only because he liked the painting but also because he knew that the artist made it valuable. Do you realize that the greatest Artist of all time made you? You are special!

Personalize these truths by saying to yourself out loud:

God made me unique.

God thinks of me constantly.

God cares for me deeply.

Right now, choose to believe these three great truths. Tell the Lord in prayer that you believe them; then thank him for personally creating you, thinking of you, and caring for you.

TAKE-AWAY THOUGHT **God's love for me is shown through his design and constant care for me.**

All I Need Is Love

Love Wants Nothing

There have been some odd inventions submitted for patents. People have come up with things that make you wonder about them (the people, that is). For example, who would be willing to purchase any of these actual inventions?

- The tapeworm trap (had to be swallowed!)
- The combined helmet, gun, and cooking pan
- The bathroom on wheels (one-seaters only)
- The mind-reading machine (this one still pops up at state fairs)
- The electric bedbug exterminator
- The spring-loaded flyswatter
- The automatic spaghetti-spinning fork
- The propeller-driven rocking chair (go, Grandpa, go!)

You think maybe these guys had a little too much free time on their hands?

Here are some other totally useless products that we hope never catch on:

- The home root-canal surgery kit (with 3/8-inch variable-speed drill)
- A screen door for your submarine
- An ejection seat for your helicopter
- The build-your-own battery-operated braces remover (batteries not included)

All right, enough of the useless products! The truth is, life is full of things you don't need. Every day in America, advertising geniuses try to persuade you to wear their shoes, chew their gum, buy their CD player, use their acne medicine, drink their soft drink, wear their jeans, hats, or sports jerseys. No one is really concerned with whether or not you actually need these things. They just want a sale. They want your money.

But when something's not practical for you, why mess with it?

In all honesty, do you ever feel that way about the Bible? When you listen to your pastor or youth leader speak, do you ever wonder, "What does that have to do with me?" or "How does something that happened thousands of years ago relate to me today?" In a sense, you're checking out the product to see if you think you need it. And sometimes your need has to be shown to you. Your job is just to keep an open heart.

So here's the question: Do you feel you need God's love?

Don't think of this in terms of a non-Christian needing salvation. Think of this question as it relates to you as a Christian.

Why do you believe you still need God's love?

Look up Ephesians 5:1-2. What are you commanded to do in verse 1?

According to the next verse, how do you do that?

What example are you given to follow as you strive to do this?

Why do you need Christ's love to do this? What's wrong with your love?

The need to receive God's love doesn't stop the moment you ask Christ to be your Savior and Lord. We all desperately need God's love on a daily basis, just as a sky diver needs a parachute. It's not an option. It's essential and practical. We need to realize our need for his love each day.

> Back in 1829, a man named George Wilson robbed a U.S. post office and killed a man in the process. Wilson was sentenced to be hanged. Fortunately for George, he had some influential friends, who petitioned President Andrew Jackson for a presidential pardon. Finally, after much persistence and persuasion, President Jackson signed the pardon. But when it was brought to Wilson, he refused to accept it!
>
> Baffled, the local sheriff didn't know what to do. He couldn't hang a pardoned man! So the matter was brought back to President Jackson, who turned the case over to the Supreme Court. After reviewing the case, Chief Justice Marshall ruled that a pardon is nothing more than a piece of paper unless it is accepted by the person for whom it is intended. In other words, a pardon refused is really not a pardon at all. So George Wilson was hanged as his pardon sat on the sheriff's desk.

Did you know that God has an unlimited supply of love, and he offers it to you every day of your life? You can have it, but you must accept it. You can apply it to your needs and your relationships each day, and the way you do this is simple.

You make God's love real in your life by choosing to follow Christ's example in the power of the Holy Spirit. You allow his power and love to flow through you. You give up your will and rights and let him love through you.

Who do you need to love today? Do you need to love someone who is

- *unlovely?*
- *unloving?*
- *unlovable?*

Remember, you can experience God's love for these people as you fully accept his love for yourself.

TAKE-AWAY THOUGHT

I need God's love in me in order to show his love to others.

CHAPTER TEN

If You Only Knew

I would always wait
For the perfect time
But now the time
Has come and gone

I hold on to the memories
As though we're still together
Longing for the strength to carry on
Ever since you've been gone

Chorus:
There's no day that goes by
I don't think of you and ask (God) why?
I won't get the chance
To tell you good-bye
And how much I lost losing you
If you only knew

Life has many pages
Some we wrote together
A story must end alone

As I go on without you
You'll live with me forever
Knowing that someday we'll meet again
Up where the rainbows end

Common Ground

If You Only Knew

:*D*uring World War I, American troops were fighting a German infantry division in the countryside of France. In the midst of the battle, a young American private became separated from his company. Afraid and lost on the battlefield, he became disoriented and couldn't remember how to get back to his fellow soldiers. Bombs exploded all around him. Dust, debris, and metal fragments were rocketing in every direction. He could hear the ricochet of bullets buzzing overhead. Finally, through the thick clouds of smoke, the private spotted a foxhole. Unsure of whose side it belonged to, he slowly made his way over, and then, with a shout, dove into the man-made ditch. To his surprise, he came face-to-face with another soldier. With guns drawn and ready to fire, the two men suddenly realized they were both wearing the same uniform. Relieved, they threw their guns down and hugged each other.

When you're on the battlefield, it always helps to be in a foxhole with someone wearing the same uniform as you. As different as soldiers might be back home, on the battlefield the differences are laid aside in order to fight together.

When two strangers find common ground, something that bonds them together, they can act like best friends in a matter of minutes. But when you think about it, isn't that what makes two people friends? Friends are people who share things in common, such as likes and dislikes, beliefs, music, sports, clothes, and hobbies. Friends usually (though not always) attend the same school and many times have classes together. On the whole, people make friends with others who are like themselves in some way. We like people who are like us.

When it comes to the world, as a Christian, you no longer have that much in common with the values and lifestyles of non-Christians. Take a look at 2 Corinthians 6:14-17, and write down as many differences between a Christian and a non-Christian as you can think of.

CHRISTIAN   NON-CHRISTIAN
•   •
•   •
•   •
•   •
•   •

What is Paul's conclusion? (v. 17)

That's why God says that being a friend with the world (that is, the world's beliefs, values, and way of living) means you are an enemy of God (James 4:4).

Even as Christians, we still have differences among us. Can you think of any differences believers might have?

Don't let these differences discourage you. Even Jesus' disciples and the first Christians had huge differences among them. There were obstacles to overcome that make our differences seem trivial by comparison. For example, some of the differences among believers in the early church were

- Jews and Gentiles
- Jews and Samaritans
- slaves and freemen
- slaves and masters
- government officials and political zealots
- former religious leaders and former prostitutes

In the early church, there were racial, social, and political differences. But the one thing they had in common was their faith in Jesus Christ. That one common bond caused them to look beyond their differences to become friends in Christ.

It's sad when we fail to see the real purpose for our relationships because we can't see past our differences. In reality, we share many things in common with our fellow Christians. According to Ephesians 4:4-6, we share the

- same body.
- same Spirit.
- same Lord.
- same faith.
- same baptism.
- same God.

We also share the same purpose in life (1 Corinthians 10:31), the same mission (Matthew 28:18-20), and the same destiny (Revelation 21:1-4). So why do we always focus on our differences instead of our similarities?

List a few of the differences between you and your Christian friends. Which one is the most difficult for you to overcome?

With the Lord's help, as far as it depends on you, choose not to allow those differences to drive a wedge between you and your friends. Remember, you're wearing the same uniform.

The most important thing about my Christian friendships is our common faith in Jesus Christ.

Stay Close Together

If You Only Knew

With their schooner safely anchored in the harbor at Owl's Head, Maine, Richard Ingraham and his fiancée, Lydia Dyer, gave little thought to the storm brewing that cold December evening. Along with their friend Roger Elliott, they weren't concerned until the anchor cables suddenly snapped, crashing the small vessel onto a reef. By this time the storm had increased in intensity, with high winds, subzero temperatures, and huge waves. With the icy waters cresting onto the deck and no possible way of escape, the three devised a last-ditch plan for survival. Lydia wrapped herself in blankets, and Richard did the same, huddling closely to her. Beside them, Roger wrapped himself in blankets too but carried a knife to carve a hole through the ice to breathe.

The following morning, Roger awoke and chipped his way through the ice to freedom. Finally making it to shore, he called for help. When rescue crews arrived, they found the couple lying together on the deck, encased in a block of ice! It took hours to slowly chip away the ice block. Then cold water was poured over them, warming up their bodies to fifty-five degrees. Miraculously, Richard and Lydia woke up and began their slow recovery back to health. Unfortunately, Roger died from frostbite. Medical personnel concluded that the couple had been saved because of the body warmth between them in spite of their near-icy grave. Six months later, they married and went on to have four children!

Sometimes it takes a crisis to realize how much we really need each other. Too often, many Christians think they can weather the storms of life alone. Unfortunately, there are too many Christians who believe they can make it by themselves in the world and in the Christian life. They fail to understand that unless we draw close to one another, we'll freeze to death out there!

Why do we need one another so much? What can we give each other as Christians? Why are our Christian friendships so important?

Look up the following verses, and see if you can discover what Christians can do for one another and why we need each other so much.

Romans 15:1

Ephesians 4:11-12 (It's through this that you learn who God is and how you can live effectively for him.)

Colossians 4:2-3

Hebrews 3:13 (This means to build up others with your words and deeds.)

1 John 1:7 (Sometimes we think we have fellowship with other Christians if we've been in the same room with them. Fellowship is more than pizza and Cokes. It's sharing our lives with one another in Christ. It's being real with each other about who we really are.)

1 John 4:7

Do you honestly think you could survive spiritually without these things from your brothers and sisters in Christ?

Psychologists have discovered that if you put a child in isolation without human touch, that child will eventually die. Why? Because God created you with a natural need to depend on others. It's just a law of life that people need people to survive. This is especially true in the Christian faith. Living your life without close Christian friends is like walking on a high wire without a net—one slip and you're history. You need others to encourage you and keep you strong in Christ.

Look back to the reasons why believers need one another. Which one of them would you say your Christian friends do for you the most?
Which one of them do you think you need right now?
Which one do you need to work on in your own life today?

TAKE-AWAY THOUGHT

I desperately need my Christian family in order to survive.

A Place Called Heaven

If You Only Knew

*B*arely making it through the front door, James collapsed on the couch and began to cry. He had just returned from his best friend's funeral and was having a really rough time. *People aren't supposed to die at seventeen,* he kept repeating in his mind. *They're supposed to live to be seventy or eighty-something.*

On their way home from a camping trip to the mountains, James and Brandon had been having a great time reliving the highlights of their trip— fishing for trout, sliding over the waterfalls, swinging on a rope and splashing into the cold mountain water, waking up in the middle of the night to find that a raccoon had eaten half their food. It had been a great trip for the two boys, who had been best friends since childhood. They couldn't wait to tell their parents all about it and get their pictures developed.

Neither James nor Brandon could have foreseen what happened next. A trucker whose brakes had gone out came around the mountain road in their lane and hit them head-on. James only suffered a broken collarbone along with some deep cuts and bruises. But because Brandon was driving, his side received the majority of the impact. After a week in a coma, Brandon died. At the funeral, the only thing that comforted James was knowing that Brandon was in heaven and that one day he would see him again.

Have you ever thought about what happens to Christians after they die? Have you ever wondered about heaven and the hereafter? Have you ever asked

- What will heaven be like?
- Who will be there?
- Will I sit on a cloud and play a harp?
- Will there be sports?

- Will there be animals?
- Will I really have a mansion?
- Will I recognize people?
- Will I see what's happening on earth?
- What age will I be in heaven?
- Will I ever be sad there?
- Will I see God?
- What will I do there?
- Will I get to ask God any question I want?
- What will I look like?

Just what do we know about heaven?

Why not let Jesus himself tell you about heaven? In John 14:1-6, Jesus dropped some pretty heavy hints about what heaven is like. In this passage, we learn several important facts about heaven. Look at Jesus' words closely and fill in the missing word.

FACT 1 Heaven is a real _____ (v. 2)

Contrary to what some religions teach, heaven is not a state of mind or a "level of consciousness." Instead, it is an actual location.

FACT 2 In heaven, Jesus is now _____ a place for me (vv. 2-3)

Think about this: Jesus spoke the universe into existence. He carefully spent six days creating the earth with its majestic mountains, rivers, gardens, and oceans. He has also spent the past two thousand years preparing a place for you. Can you even imagine how great heaven is going to be?

FACT 3 Heaven is where _____ is (v. 3)

Jesus told his friends that he was going away for a while but that he would return and bring them to be with him. The Bible teaches us that when we die (or when Jesus returns) we will be reunited with every loved one who has died in the Lord. Death is a separation, and heaven is a reunion. It's like the little girl who asked her grandfather, "Will we know each other when we get to heaven?" "Sweetheart," the wise old man chuckled, "we won't really know each other until we get to heaven."

FACT 4 The only way to heaven is through _____ (vv. 4-6)

Only Christ paid the penalty for our sin. Only he rose from the dead. Only Jesus made a bridge between humankind and God. No other religious leader could ever make those claims. Not Buddha. Not Muhammad. Not Confucius. Not Abraham. Only Jesus.

Though it's not mentioned in this passage, we know from other Scriptures that there will be no sickness, suffering, sadness, sin, pain, worry, crying, or death (Revelation 21:4).

Back when trains were the fastest way to travel from coast to coast, a little boy was riding from Missouri to California to spend the summer with his father. It was a hot and dusty day as the train pulled out of the station. The ride would prove to be quite uncomfortable over the next few days. But the little boy sat quietly in his seat, not saying a word. Finally, a motherly woman leaned over and said to the boy, "Son, aren't you tired of this long ride, with all the dust and the heat?" The little boy looked up with a smile and said, "Yes, ma'am, a little. But I don't mind the journey. You see, my father is going to meet me at the other end."

Heaven is your home. This earth is just a glorified hotel. Your journey has an end. One day, you will go to your heavenly home with no stops in between. Your ticket has been purchased by Christ on the cross. Heaven will be a place that has been prepared for you by Jesus himself. And your heavenly Father will be waiting for you at the end of your journey, along with all those who have made the journey ahead of you.

What's the one thing about heaven you are looking forward to?

It's never easy to say good-bye to someone you love, especially when someone close to you has died and gone on to heaven. But remember, Christians never really say good-bye, they just say so long.
Is there someone you're longing to see in heaven?
Remember, you'll see them again.

One day I will be with Jesus and reunited with my loved ones in heaven.

You Don't Know What You've Got Until...

DAY 43

If You Only Knew

In 1765, an illegitimate son named James Smithson was born to an English duke in France. But because Smithson was born out of wedlock, he was refused British citizenship and denied an inheritance from his rich father. In spite of this, James was determined to succeed at whatever he did. Pursuing the study of science, he became one of England's leading scientists by the age of twenty-two. In 1829, Smithson died. The English scientific community hoped they would receive a large financial grant from the great scientist's estate. But in his will, Smithson had written: "Just as England has rejected me, so I have rejected England." To show his contempt for England for not recognizing and appreciating him, James gave a fortune to that upstart former colony, the United States! The American government took the money and established a scientific institution, calling it the Smithsonian Institute. England made a huge mistake when it failed to appreciate James Smithson. They simply weren't grateful for what they had.

That's an appropriate illustration for us as Christians. God brings people into our lives, and many times we don't appreciate them for who they are until they're gone. Isn't it strange that we wait until someone's funeral to say really nice things about them? It seems that when a person is gone—either moves away or dies—we suddenly realize how much that person meant to us. Unfortunately, it is only then that we recognize the person's worth and value to us as well as his or her contribution to our lives.

Why not change all that and start appreciating people now instead of later? Take a look at how Paul practiced this kind of gratefulness in his life. Look up the following verses, and see what he said about his friends and why he was so thankful for them.

	WHAT PAUL SAID	WHY HE SAID IT
• Romans 1:8	•	•
• Philippians 1:3, 5-7	•	•
• Colossians 1:3-5	•	•
• 1 Thessalonians 1:2-6	•	•

Paul was a very busy man. He traveled a lot and had a lot of responsibility. Yet he found time to sit down and write letters to different believers to encourage them and to express his gratitude for them.

How do you think Paul's friends felt when they received his letters of praise and encouragement?

What do you think it did for their relationship with Paul?

There's something about losing things that makes you want them more. For example, you don't know how much

- your freedom means to you until you're grounded for the weekend.
- your car means to you until your parents take away the keys.
- your health means to you until you get sick riding on a bus.
- your clear complexion means to you until you break out right before a big date.
- your best friend means to you until you find out his family is moving.
- your money means to you until you realize you're broke.
- your playing time means to you until you're benched.
- your music means to you until your stereo finally breaks down.

So it's really true that "You don't know what you've got until it's gone."

Though it's not a pleasant thought, have you ever pictured what your life would be like without those closest to you, like your parents, relatives, or best friends? When is the last time you thanked

- your parents for all they do for you?
- your pastor for all his hard work?
- your youth pastor for his ministry to you?
- your Christian friends for being an encouragement to you?
- your grandparents for their love for you?
- your Sunday-school teachers or other church leaders for teaching you?
- your brothers or sisters for putting up with you?

Are there people in your life who you take for granted? Write down a few names, then jot down one or two reasons why they mean so much to you.

Name	He or she means a lot to me because
_____	_____
_____	_____
_____	_____
_____	_____
_____	_____

To help you put God's Word into practice, why not write a short note to each of these people, expressing your appreciation for them?

I need to appreciate and encourage my friends and family now, not later.

Taming the Wild Beast

If You Only Knew

If you've ever been through a tornado, you know the incredible power and destruction fierce acts of nature can bring. On the lighter side is the humorous nature of tornadoes. According to the American Meteorological Society, pieces of paper have been known to travel more than two hundred miles inside tornadoes. Big deal, right? Maybe, but what about these tornado tidbits:

- In 1913, a pillow traveled twenty miles in an Alabama storm.
- A cow was carried ten miles by an Iowa tornado in 1978 (it was "moooo"-ved).
- A headstone was transported three miles in a Minnesota twister.
- Once, a crate containing deer hides flew six miles (Rudolph, is that you?).
- In 1927, a jar of pickles traveled eighteen miles in Indiana.
- A sack of flour in Kansas was picked up and moved one hundred miles in 1915.

Wind has awesome power. But the Bible talks about something that has even more power than a twister. It can bring more devastation into a life than any storm of nature. In fact, it's so powerful that nations have fallen because of it. Homes have been wrecked from its deadly force. Relationships have been destroyed because of its fury. People have a hard time taming its force, and its wrath is totally unpredictable.

What is this dreaded creature? Look up James 3:7-8 and find out.

Now that you know what it is, see what you can find out about the tongue in verses 2-12.

What is the tongue compared to in the following verses?

- Verse 3
- Verse 4
- Verses 5-6

One spark of fire can destroy an entire forest. And one word can start a fire in a friendship or a family, igniting a blaze that can destroy a person. Whoever said "Sticks and stones will break my bones, but words can never harm me" was dead wrong! Words don't break bones—they break hearts.

How else does James describe the tongue? (vv. 7-8)

Think about it. James is saying that you would have a better chance taming a wild lion than you would have taming your tongue!

Why do you think words have such a powerful influence?

Sometimes our tongue shifts into high gear before our head can catch up with it. Remember, every time you open your mouth, you show what's in your heart. Your words can hurt, or they can heal. They can harm another person, or they can be used to help him or her. When you cut someone else down with your words, it's usually to make yourself look good. You can never take back your words once you've spoken them. So make sure you mean what you say and that what you say is valuable. A good rule to live by is to talk about other people the way you would want them to talk about you.

On May 21, 1941, the German battleship *Bismarck* was sighted in the North Atlantic. As the battleship frantically made her way toward German-controlled France, she suddenly made a 180-degree turn and headed back out to sea toward the British ships that were chasing her. The *Bismarck* began to steer a zigzag course, which slowed her down considerably. The British ships closed in and sank the mighty *Bismarck*, sending her to the bottom of the Atlantic Ocean. It was later learned that a torpedo had damaged the *Bismarck's* rudder, which explained the erratic course that led to her sinking.

It's the same way with our tongues. If our "rudder" is damaged, then our "ship" will sink. A damaged tongue uses unkind words or profanity. It's a tongue that tears people down instead of building them up. Yesterday you learned about appreciating the ones who are closest to you. You found out how you could show your gratitude to them. One way to do that is in your daily conversations with them. Keep in mind that your words can be medicine or they can be poison.

If someone paid you ten dollars for every kind word you spoke over the next six months, but collected five dollars for every unkind word you spoke, would you be rich or poor at the end of that time?

What final point does James make about the tongue? (vv. 9-12)

What do you think is the key to taming your tongue?

I need to allow Christ to control my tongue so that I will speak kind words to others.

Don't Stop Now!
If You Only Knew

Howard Hughes was one of the richest men in America. Born into a wealthy family, Hughes never lacked for money or material possessions. By the time he was nineteen, he was a millionaire in his own right. He continued in his father's business for several years until his interests turned to Hollywood. Because he didn't like the way some studios were producing movies, he bought a studio and began making his own movies. Hughes also loved flying, so he became a pilot and bought his own airline. By 1938, he was a national hero, setting world speed records. In the 1940s, Hughes built the largest plane in the world. Called the *Spruce Goose* because it was made mostly of wood, this massive plane had a 360-foot wing span, weighed several thousand tons, and cost a whopping eighteen million dollars to build. Because of the length of time it took to build the plane plus its enormous size, people speculated that it would never fly. At last in 1947, with Hughes at the controls, the world's largest plane took off over the water and flew for forty-five seconds. It flew for a distance of only about a mile, then the *Spruce Goose* landed and was stored in a hangar, never to fly again.

There are a lot of similarities between the *Spruce Goose* and some Christians—both are impressive on the outside, but when put to the test don't last very long. For some people, their faith just doesn't last. Their faith fizzles out. They might begin well, but like that plane, these people can't sustain the altitude for long. Why not?

Basically, there's too much pull from below and not enough power from the engine *within*.

In a way, by devoting the last forty-four days to your relationship with God and his Word, you've made a commitment of sorts to keep going. And you probably don't want it to stop here, do you? You want to go on. To stay airborne and become a long-term Christian. So how can you do that?

In Mark 4:1-9, Jesus told his disciples a parable about four kinds of soils that represent four different people and their hearts, or spiritual conditions. Out of the four, only one lasts. In verses 10-20, Jesus goes on to explain why. Let's take a closer look at each heart.

1. The Hardened Heart (vv. 3-4)
   What happens to this person? (vv. 14-15)

Bottom line: This person doesn't listen to the Word.

2. The Shallow Heart (vv. 5-6)
   Why doesn't this person last? (vv. 16-17)

Bottom line: This person has no roots.

3. The Divided Heart (v. 7)
   What keeps this person from a commitment to God? (vv. 18-19)

Bottom line: This person has no loyalty.

4. The Fruitful Heart (vv. 8-9)
   Why is this heart different from the other ones? (v. 20)

Bottom line: This person allows the Word to rule in his or her life.

Four hearts. One seed (the Word). Four different responses. Four different results. The big question is, Which one is going to describe you? Which kind of heart will you have? And how will you make sure that you keep going strong?

> **Shortly after World War I, Lawrence of Arabia was in Paris with some of his Arab friends. After seeing the Louvre, the Arch of Triumph, and Napoleon's tomb, his friends hardly seemed impressed. But one thing really sparked their interest more than anything else—the faucet in the bathtub of their hotel room. They spent hours turning it on and off, amazed at how it worked. By just turning a handle, they could have all the water they wanted. When it was time to leave, Lawrence discovered his friends in the bathroom with a wrench, trying to detach the faucet. They explained to him, "In Arabia, it is very dry. But if we have this faucet, we will have all the water we need!" Lawrence had to persuade them that the power of the faucets did not come from themselves, but from the immense system of waterworks to which they were attached. The water ultimately came from the rain and snowfall in the Alps.**

It's the same way for you. Your power to continue on in your Christian life does not come from you or depend upon you. You have a faucet, but you must make sure it is connected to the spiritual pipeline each day. Your power comes from above; you must rely on *his* resources, not your own. This is something you must choose to do every day.

What are some ways to make sure you'll keep spending time with God each day? Write down some ideas you have.

Close by spending some time in prayer. Ask God to help you have a fruitful heart as you spend time with him daily. Write a short note of commitment to the Lord, telling him about your desire to keep going strong in your walk with him. You might also want to ask a friend to hold you accountable to your devotions as you make this a consistent part of your life.

To keep going spiritually each day, I must stay connected to Christ and draw my strength from him.

Forty-Five Awesome Principles to Live By

1. I need to remember that God loves me and sent his Son for me!
2. I need to keep my relationship with Christ simple and clutter-free.
3. I can worship God by living a life that brings honor to him.
4. Prayer is talking to God and having fellowship with him.
5. Because of Jesus, I can go to God in prayer anytime.
6. To communicate with God, I must maintain a clear connection in prayer.
7. One of the greatest things I can do for someone else is to faithfully pray for him or her.
8. Understanding what God says about the future of the world will help me live for him in the present.
9. Pleasing God has to be my highest priority.
10. When my beliefs cost me, I can stand strong with other Christians and with God on my side.
11. When I stand for Christ, he stands with me.
12. Problems are part of life. I'm not alone, because all Christians go through struggles.
13. When I face problems, I can run to the Lord for strength and safety.
14. When I am hurting and confused about life, I should share my struggles with a Christian friend.
15. When I keep my priorities in order, I will experience joy and God's blessing in my life.
16. I must never give up following Christ, no matter what happens.
17. When I am committed to spiritual growth, my faith becomes my own.

18. I am not the person I used to be. God has made me into a new person!

19. Together, my Christian friends and I can have a huge influence for God on our campus.

20. I can leave a legacy of faith to those behind me.

21. I should never stop bringing others to Jesus.

22. Jesus demands all of me if I want to call myself his disciple.

23. It's a serious thing to follow Christ, so I must count the cost.

24. If I hear and obey Christ's words, I can face any storm life dumps on me.

25. The more I seek to know Jesus in a personal way each day, the more I avoid spiritual phoniness.

26. I shouldn't hesitate to have faith in God, because he can be trusted with every area of my life.

27. I must pay attention to the little choices I make because every decision is important and has consequences.

28. I must consider the consequences of my choices before I make them.

29. As I make choices, I can depend on the wisdom from God's Word to guide me.

30. In order to live a life that's different, I must seek to please God in all I do.

31. Jesus offers me a relationship that is extremely hip and that truly satisfies.

32. Jesus satisfies me and meets my every need.

33. Through Jesus, I find my way to happiness, hope, and heaven.

34. By depending on God's strength, I can live above my circumstances.

35. God's love for me is totally faithful and infinite.

36. God loves me even though I don't deserve it.

37. God's love satisfies and fulfills me like nothing else can.

38. God's love for me is shown through his design and constant care for me.

39. I need God's love in me in order to show his love to others.

40. The most important thing about my Christian friendships is our common faith in Jesus Christ.

41. I desperately need my Christian family in order to survive.

42. One day I will be with Jesus and reunited with my loved ones in heaven.

43. I need to appreciate and encourage my friends and family now, not later.

44. I need to allow Christ to control my tongue so that I will speak kind words to others.

45. To keep going spiritually each day, I must stay connected to Christ and draw my strength from him.

More about Al Denson

There is a different kind of music playing in Al Denson's life these days. It's more than just the normal melodies of a singer, songwriter, and author. It is the song of testimony to God's grace demonstrated in his life. We call it "a God thing." Al can no longer be content with past accomplishments. A traumatic journey has clarified his mission, empowered his testimony, and changed the music deep within his soul.

In December 1994, Al was involved in a plane crash that took the life of his friend Grant Milner. By God's grace, Al survived. But he suffered the emotional and physical loss of his friend and the trauma of reconstructive surgery and lengthy recovery. Thousands of letters flooded Celebration Ministries with prayers of hope and encouragement. The church began to minister healing back into the life of this man. The crash impacted the entire ministry and its organization and has changed the direction of Al's career. In fact, it has pointed Al more formally to the relevance of the church as the body of Christ, of every person's individual walk with Christ, and of the gospel as the cornerstone for our faith.

Who is Al Denson? He's a young man who has been broken.

Bill Baumgart of Benson Music Group states, "Just a month or two before Al's greatest physical challenge, Al really began to focus on his personal walk with Christ. He was taking everything that didn't fit in his artistry and ministry, and redirecting the focus with complete accountability and spiritual discipline. It was as if God still wanted more of his life."

Al explains, "Scripture says to 'wait on the Lord,' and it seems that sometimes I've lived whole segments of my life as if I'd just torn that out of my Bible. It's funny, because God has been taking a chisel to mold me, but I wouldn't let him swing the instrument. You know it can really hurt. Now, I'm just letting God begin to take more swings, and even though it hurts, you sure feel better for it because you know it's from him. It's making a difference in what I do and how my artistry and ministry is shaped."

Under the direction of Celebration Ministries and its board of advisers, Al is seeking to raise the standards in the Christian music industry for integrity, prayer, the place of the Word of God, and personal relationships. With a heart toward integrity and the preaching of the gospel, Al has made accountability and hard work cornerstones of his ministry. Currently, Celebration Ministries is focused on building a prayer team of people from every walk of life and evangelical denomination. Al believes that prayer is what will make the difference in a vibrant ministry. Thousands of Bibles are given away each year as people are pointed to the Bible as God's perfect word of hope and salvation. Al's love for his wife, Tracie, has encouraged him to be more committed to living out the reality of God's love in their relationship.

Prior to the accident, Al Denson was blessed to have been involved in ministry with powerful Christian leaders from across the country. From his early ministry with Dawson McAlister to his present ministry with the Billy Graham Evangelistic Association and Franklin Graham, the ministry partnerships have played a vital role in evangelism and discipleship training in his ministry.

Al has traveled to Bosnia with Franklin Graham's Samaritan's Purse organization as part of Operation Christmas Child, their unique program of giving. This incredible program encourages the children of a dangerous and forgotten land. The team distributed shoeboxes filled with small gifts, basic school supplies, and personal hygiene items to almost one million children in this war-torn country.

Al's concerts demonstrate a heart for ministry and a passion to see people come to know Christ as Lord and Savior. He spends time after each concert to find out what young people think, to understand how they believe, and to point them to the "right choices." Because of his direct approach and unique perspective, young people who might be considered outside the lines of Christian circles will listen to the message he carries.

The lessons of his personal journey may be found in the album *Take Me to the Cross*. "I'm in the process of growing up—not just in maturity, but with my relationship with Christ," Al relates. "Some of the things that I've heard and read and had instilled in me all of my life, I have experienced and know really work." The forty-five-day companion devotional is a natural outgrowth of the process and his burden for discipleship. He says, "We can't just take lyrics and stop there, because there is a reason for these words that breathes life." Al concludes, "My prayer every day is that I wake up in a position of need. In fact, we began this project on our knees, and we want to finish this project in the same place. It's a place where I have to meet God personally just to make life happen."

Our prayer is that Jesus Christ alone will receive all of the glory and that you will be different because you have come to know him.

Kevin McAfee
Celebration Ministries

OPERATION CHRISTMAS CHILD

Operation Christmas Child is a project of Samaritan's Purse, an international Christian relief and evangelism organization. This unique project sends a message of hope to children in desperate situations around the world through gift-filled shoe boxes, relief aid, and Christian literature.

Operation Christmas Child provides an opportunity for individuals of all ages to be involved in a simple, hands-on missions project that reaches out to needy children while focusing on the true meaning of Christmas—Jesus Christ, God's greatest gift.

Every year thousands of churches, schools, and organizations around the world participate in Operation Christmas Child. Last year we collected over one million shoe boxes from across the United States, Canada, Europe, and Australia and distributed them to children in dozens of countries throughout Latin America, Eastern Europe, Africa, Asia, and the Middle East.

How to Fill a Shoe Box

 Find an empty shoe box. You can wrap it—lid separately—if you would like, but wrapping is not required.

 Determine whether your gift will be for a boy or girl and the age category: Infant, (2–4), (5–9), or (10–14). Place the appropriate boy/girl sticker from your brochure on the TOP of your box and mark the correct age category.

 Fill your shoe box with a variety of gifts from the following categories:

- Small toys: stuffed animals, dolls, balls, cars, etc.
  (No toy guns, knives, or other war-related items, please)

- School supplies: pens, pencils/sharpener, crayons, coloring books, writing pads/paper, solar calculator

- Hygiene items: toothbrush, toothpaste, soap, comb/brush

- Other: T-shirts, socks, Bible-story picture books, sealed hard candy/gum *(No other food items, please)*
  Please do not include items that may easily break or leak.

 You may enclose a note to the child and a photo of yourself or your family. *(If you include your name and address, the child who receives your box may write to you.)*

Enclose **$5** or more in the envelope from your brochure and place it in your shoe box to help cover shipping and other costs related to Operation Christmas Child. **(Checks are recommended rather than cash. If you or your family are filling more than one shoe box, you may make one combined donation in a single envelope and place it inside any one of your boxes.)** Place a rubber band around your shoe box and lid.

 For shipping and collection information, or if you have any other questions, call 1-800-353-5949.